INTERMEDIATE B1+

by James Styring and Alastair Lane

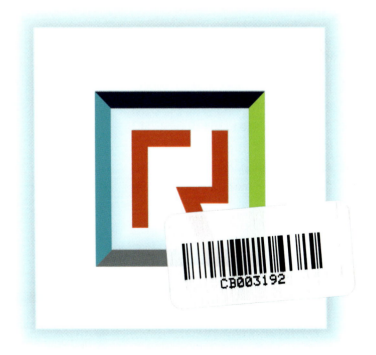

Richmond Mazes are fun, interactive readers set in a variety of interesting contexts. As you read you have to make decisions and choose how the story develops. These are enjoyable and effective ways to learn and practise English wherever you are.

What they include:

- Engaging, fun stories to keep readers entertained for hours
- Graded language to suit students at all levels
- An interactive approach which puts the reader in control of how the stories develop
- A range of lively characters and surprising storylines
- A rich mixture of audio and colour illustrations which brings the stories to life
- A glossary section to check the meaning of all business vocabulary
- Lots of opportunity to re-read the story making different decisions and finding new routes through the maze

See if you can find your way through the maze!

This story and other Richmond Mazes can also be downloaded onto Apple and Android devices. Available from the iTunes App Store and Google Play.

Crisis at Clifton

In this fun, interactive reader you will learn and practise business English.
The goal is to save the Clifton Creative Agency, but to do this you must make the correct decisions.

▶ section 1   Read the story carefully, look at the different options and then turn to the correct section to make your decision.

You can win bonus points as you move through the story. If you win a bonus point, mark it on the scorecard on page 186.

◀ section 1   If you make a bad decision, you will have to start the chapter again.

 Sometimes you have to write down important information. If you see this symbol, write down the information on page 186.

 You can listen to the audio at **www.richmondelt.com/international/ resources/richmond-mazes**

suburb*   You can check the meaning of words with this symbol in the glossary on page 187.

Good luck!

Chapter 1

Section 1

It is spring in Australia. The sun is shining and it is a beautiful day in the Sydney suburb* of Manly. In the street outside, people are smiling and chatting happily. Everyone seems cheerful* ... everyone except you! You are nervous – very nervous, because you are sitting in the reception of Clifton Creative Agency and today is the first day of your new job.

The staff* at Clifton are young and trendy*. As you sit in reception, you watch people walking past wearing slim-fit jeans, cool* glasses and fashionable clothes. It feels like a very different world from your last job in the auto industry*, and you feel slightly out of place.

Then you remember why Clifton gave you the job. Their biggest client* is a car company – Avoca Autos. In your last job, you were head of brand* advertising for a major Australian car manufacturer and you commissioned* advertising agencies to create your company's car adverts. Bored of your old position, you decided to look for a more creative job in advertising. Now you are an account director at Clifton – you will manage the agency's relationships with their clients. 'Everything's going to be OK,' you think. 'I'm not an expert in advertising, but I do know about the car business. Clifton needs me.'

While you are waiting in reception, you hear a lot of noise coming from the offices. Suddenly a door opens, and a man comes out. He has curly black hair which is a little grey at the sides. He is wearing a smart

Chapter 1

dark suit. He seems stressed* and he walks up and down, talking under his breath. Then he takes a piece of gum* out of his pocket and starts chewing* it, angrily.

Do you …

1 introduce yourself? ▶ section 2

2 wait to see what happens? ▶ section 3

2 Section 2

'Er … excuse me,' you say.

'Can I help you?' the man asks. He comes closer to you. There is a security card on his jacket. Reading it, you see that his name is 'John Miller' and that he works for Clifton. This man is one of your new colleagues*.

'Oh, we're going to be working together,' you say. You tell him your name.

'Oh, yes,' says John. 'Welcome to Clifton. I'm John Miller.'

You shake hands. His handshake* is very hard – too hard, and you feel slightly uncomfortable. At last, he takes his hand away. 'I'm an account director, too,' says John.

'I'm pleased to meet you,' you say.

Strangely, John does not respond. He scratches* his head and chews his gum noisily. 'Come inside and meet the team,' he says. 'I hope you're ready for this job because we have a very busy day in front of us.' He swipes* his security card and the glass doors to Clifton's offices open. You follow him inside. As you walk down the corridor together, you have the opportunity to make small talk* with John.

What do you say?

1 'How did you get into the advertising business, John?' ▶ section 7

2 'So, John, how's everything going at Clifton?' ▶ section 8

Chapter 1

Section 3

The man walks up and down, scratches* his head and talks angrily to himself. You think about introducing yourself, but in the end you decide to stay on the sofa. Finally, the man goes back through the doors into the office. He nearly walks into a woman who is coming out. 'Sorry, Sylvia,' he mutters* and then he goes through the door.

You recognise* her. She is Sylvia, the office manager. You met her at your interview. 'Hello,' she says. 'It's so nice to see you again. Welcome to Clifton.'

'Thank you, Sylvia,' you say. 'I'm very excited to be here.'

'Shall we go in?' Sylvia asks. She swipes* her security card and the door opens. As you walk down the corridor together, you have the opportunity to make small talk* with her.

Section 4

Sylvia shakes* her head. 'That's a very good question!' she says. 'The company's been very successful over the years, but recently, we've started to get worried. There are lots of new agencies opening and they all want a piece of our business.'

'Is the company in danger?'

'I don't know,' says Sylvia. 'You'll have to ask Karen that, but I do know that the company needs new ideas. When we heard that you were going to start, everyone was talking about it. Why should the company recruit* an outsider* from the car industry? Nobody understood it.'

You are not sure what to say. Sylvia changes the subject. She chats about her home life. She is very friendly and she tells you about her teenage son. Apparently, she lives alone with him.

Finally, she opens the door of an office. 'This is Karen Booth's office.'

Chapter 1

5 Section 5

⭐ You win 1 bonus point. Mark the scorecard on page 186.

'That was John Miller,' says Sylvia quietly. 'He's another account director. He does the same job as you. Between you and me, he isn't happy that you've got this job.'

'Why's that?' you ask.

'John's worried about his own job. He thinks that the company wants to replace* him – with you!'

'Oh,' you say.

'So be careful, there's a lot of competition in this business. Not everyone is your friend.'

You have learned a useful piece of information!

After that, you chat about Sylvia's life. You guess* she is about forty-five. She is very friendly and she tells you about her teenage son. Apparently, she lives alone with him.

Finally, she opens an office door. 'This is Karen Booth's office.'

▶ section 6

6 Section 6

So far, you have been very impressed* with the Clifton office. It is bright with glass walls and modern art everywhere. You both go into a meeting room at the end of the corridor. Inside, there is a large flat screen TV. A woman in a business suit is watching it and she doesn't look happy. You recognise* her immediately* from your interview. She is Karen Booth, your new boss. She smiles and invites you to sit down.

8

Chapter 1

Karen introduces you to the other members of the team in the room. 'So here we all are,' she says. 'Let me introduce you. As you know, I'm Karen Booth and I'm your line manager*, so you'll be reporting to me.'

'Yes,' you say.

'Next to you is John Miller. He's an account director as well. Like you, he manages the relationship with our clients.'

'It's not an easy job,' says John.

'Er … yes,' continues Karen. 'And finally, we have Sylvia Watson. Sylvia is the office manager and she's responsible for stationery*, making appointments*, contracts and general admin work.'

'Basically, if you have a problem, ask me,' says Sylvia with a smile.

'Nice to meet you all,' you say. 'I'm really pleased to be working here.'

'That's good news,' says Karen. 'But, unfortunately, today is going to be difficult.'

'Oh. What's wrong?' you ask.

Section 7

'Well, unlike some people, I have a degree* in advertising,' says John. 'I also worked for seven years as a copywriter*, before I became an account director. I have more than fifteen years' experience in advertising.'

'You were a copywriter,' you say. 'What adverts did you work on?'

'Listen,' John says. 'We don't say "advert", we just say "ad". You're inside the business now. You need to talk the talk. Right, we're here. Time to meet Karen.' He stares* at you. 'Our boss.'

Section 8

'Personally,' says John, 'I think things are fine at Clifton. To be honest, I don't understand why they recruited* a new account director.'

You realise that John is talking about you. 'They told me that the company is worried about a contract* with a car company,' you reply. 'I worked in the auto industry for many years.'

'Making cars is very different to selling them,' says John. 'Advertising is a creative business. You need big ideas. Anyway, we're here. Let's go and meet Karen.' He stares* at you. 'Our boss.'

9

Chapter 1

9 Section 9

'Watch this,' Karen says and turns on the TV. You recognise the programme. It is a popular Australian soap opera*.

'This is awful*,' says Sylvia.

John says nothing. He taps* his fingers on the desk and keeps on chewing a piece of gum.

What do you say?

1 'What's wrong with it?' ▶ section 10

2 'I agree! It's the worst thing on TV at the moment. Why do they make rubbish like this?' ▶ section 11

10 Section 10

Quickly, Karen explains. Avoca Autos is the company's biggest client. They sponsor* the soap opera on Australian TV. This means that there is a message from Avoca Autos before, during and after the show. The viewers all see a strong connection between the show and the cars. Last night's show had an accident where a car caught fire on an Australian highway* and burnt. It was an Avoca car! Everyone looks at you.

'What do you think we should do?' asks Karen.

What do you say?

1 'We should complain to the TV company and apologise to Avoca Autos.' ▶ section 13

2 'Don't worry about it. Most people won't notice the car.' ▶ section 12

Chapter 1

Section 11

Sylvia stares at you. She looks quite shocked*.

Karen's face goes red. 'I hope you never speak like that in front of our clients,' she says. 'We spend a huge* amount of money sponsoring* this show.'

'If you want to be successful in this business,' says John, 'you have to understand how the public think. People love this show. They love soap operas. Maybe you don't understand the public very well.'

There is an uncomfortable silence in the room.

'So, what's the problem?' you ask.

Section 12

John Miller answers. 'If people don't notice the cars,' he says, 'why do we pay to sponsor the show?'

'Er …' you say.

'And, unfortunately*,' adds Karen, 'thanks to social media, more and more people will notice our advertising mistakes*. Everyone is tweeting*, about the TV show and Avoca. They're laughing at us!'

'That's right,' says John. 'You have a lot to learn about this business.'

'Well, let's get to work. We need to solve this crisis*,' says Karen. 'Sylvia, get me the phone number of our contact at the TV station. John, you go and phone Hans at Avoca to explain the situation and say sorry.'

Everyone gets up. Karen turns to you. She looks worried. 'Could you come and see me at 3.00 this afternoon?' she asks. 'We need to have a chat about the company and your role with us.'

'OK, I'll see you at 3.00,' you reply. You are relieved that the meeting has finished because it was hard to know the best thing to say.

Section 13

'Yes, I absolutely agree,' says Karen. 'I think we have to take this situation very seriously. I'll contact the TV company myself.'

Chapter 1

> **What do you say?**
>
> 1 'We should also ask the TV company to give Avoca some free air time.' ▶ section 17
>
> 2 'How did this happen? Don't we see the scripts for the programme?' ▶ section 18

14 Section 14

Quickly, Karen explains. Avoca Autos is the company's biggest client. They sponsor the soap opera on Australian TV. This means that there is a message from Avoca Autos before, during and after the show. The viewers all see a strong connection between the show and the cars. Last night's show had an accident where a car caught fire on an Australian highway* and burnt. It was an Avoca car! Everyone looks at you.

'What do you think we should do?' asks Karen.

> **What do you say?**
>
> 1 'We should complain to the TV company and apologise to Avoca Autos.' ▶ section 13
>
> 2 'Pretend that nothing has happened. No one will notice the broken down car.' ▶ section 15

15 Section 15

'Let me get this straight,' says Karen. 'You think that no one notices the cars in these TV programmes. Our clients pay tens of thousands of dollars to sponsor the show. Are you saying that they are wasting* their money?'

There is another uncomfortable silence in the room.

'Honestly!' says John to you. 'What's the point? It's obvious that you have no feeling for this business. What were you thinking, Karen? Is this the person that's going to save Clifton?'

Sylvia doesn't look at you. Karen nods her head. 'Can I speak to you in private?' she asks.

▶ section 19

Chapter 1

Section 16

At 3.00 you go to Karen Booth's office. Once the door is closed, she smiles and offers you a coffee. You notice that she is drinking green tea. Its unusual smell fills the room. 'Thank you for helping today,' she says. 'And I'm sorry that I put you on the spot about Avoca Autos. The thing is, we really need your industry knowledge. Clifton is in trouble.'

'I thought the company was very successful,' you say.

'We are successful, but it's all down to Pareto's Principle.'

'Pareto's Principle?' you ask.

'Yes. It's a law that says things divide 80–20. In Clifton's case, 80% of our profits* come from 20% of our clients. We have two big clients and one of them is Avoca Autos.'

'So the problem with the soap opera was serious?'

'Absolutely,' Karen agrees. 'We're in the last six months of a three-year contract with Avoca Autos. It's essential* that they renew* that contract. That's why you're here. You're an expert in the car industry and you know what they want from advertisers.'

'That's true,' you say.

'We're about to start an advertising campaign* for the new Avoca Arrow. It's a small 4x4 car.' Karen drinks some of her tea. 'They want a big campaign and you're going to run* it, with John Miller.'

'Wow! I *think* I can do that,' you say.

'I must emphasise* that our company is in crisis. If we fail and we lose the Avoca contract, we will go out of business.'

'I understand,' you say.

'And as you know, you're on a probationary* period for six months,' says Karen. 'That means if things go badly, we can ask you to leave.'

'Yes, I understand,' you say. 'That's normal in this business.'

'OK, good luck,' says Karen. 'The survival of our company is in your hands.'

Section 17

'Excellent suggestion,' says Karen. What do you think, John?'

'Pah!' he says. 'The TV company won't give Avoca any free air time*.'

Chapter 1

'We'll see about that,' says Karen. 'Sylvia, get me the phone number of our contact at the TV station. John, you phone Hans at Avoca to explain the situation and say sorry.' Karen looks at you. 'I'm really pleased we have you on the team. Come and see me at 3.00 today and we'll have a chat about your role in the company.'

18 Section 18

'We do see the scripts*,' says Karen. 'Who reads them?'

'That's your job isn't it, John?' says Sylvia.

John Miller's face goes white and he stops chewing his gum. 'I ... yes, well, I usually read all the scripts, but I've been so busy with the Avoca Arrow that I didn't notice the storyline about the car on fire ...'

'I see,' says Karen. 'Well, let's make some phone calls and try to fix* the problem. I'll phone the TV company to complain* and John, you call Hans at Avoca. He needs to know we're taking this seriously.' Karen turns to you. 'Could you come and see me at 3.00 this afternoon?' she asks. 'We need to have a chat about your role in the company.'

As you go out, John gives you a very angry look. 'I'll remember this,' he says.

19 Section 19

You follow Karen into her office, where she gives you some bad news. 'I'm very sorry,' she says, 'but I'm afraid that John's right. It doesn't look like this is the career* for you. Perhaps there's still time to get your old job back.'

'Isn't there anything I can do?' you ask.

Karen shakes her head sadly. 'I'm very sorry, but I'm afraid this is where we say goodbye,' she says, as she stands up.

'Goodbye,' you sigh.

Your career in advertising has lasted 25 minutes!

Go back to the start of the chapter and try again.

Chapter 2

Section 20

Despite your lack* of experience in advertising, your boss Karen expects* you to produce some incredible results. You know you have a lot to learn, and if every day at Clifton is as stressful* as yesterday, you want to make sure you are prepared.

You arrive at 7.20 a.m. and the sun is hot on your back as you walk from the car park to the Clifton offices. Inside, the building is dark and the air con feels fresh on your skin. As you walk past reception, you bump into* Sylvia.

'Good morning!' she says with a smile. 'The early bird catches the worm, eh?'

'Sorry?' you ask. You are distracted. You have been thinking about the day ahead. You were not expecting a friendly chat this early in the morning.

'I said, the early bird catches the worm. You must have a lot to do today.'

'Yes, I've been thinking about it all in the car.'

'Fancy a quick coffee before you start?'

Section 21

'There's something I should tell you,' says Sylvia, 'while no one else is here.' She swipes* her security card and you enter the open-plan* office.

'Really? What's that?' you ask. You walk over to the coffee machine. 'What are you having?' you ask.

'Decaf cappuccino, please,' Sylvia says.

You place a mug* on a tray in the machine and push a button. The mug fills with hot coffee and milk. You get yourself an Americano.

'Thanks,' says Sylvia, blowing steam* from the mug. 'It's about John.'

Chapter 2

'John Miller?'

'Yes. One of the reasons that Karen's employed you is that John is having problems. He's been working on the Avoca account for months and he can't get them to commit* to anything. We've had three-year contracts* with Avoca for a long time. The current* contract expires* in six months and Karen's worried that they will leave us unless we can produce a great campaign* for their new car.'

'Oh, right. Thanks for the tip.' This is definitely interesting information, although you are rather surprised that Sylvia has told you this. You chat for five minutes before going to your desk.

▶ section 26

22 Section 22

You spend the next couple of hours working at your desk. You read a lot of background* information about Avoca's other cars and you look at the campaigns that Clifton ran for those vehicles. After that, you meet a few of the junior account handlers and have a coffee.

Finally, at 11.15, John comes into the office. He looks very hot. 'Sorry I'm late!' he says. 'Coffee?'

'No thanks. I've just had one.'

John disappears and a young woman walks in without knocking.

'Hi!' she says. 'My name's Layla. Layla Evans. You must be the new account director. Nice to meet you. I'm the copywriter* you and John will be working with on the Arrow campaign. Well – you'll be working, I'm not so sure about John!' She laughs.

Layla seems very self-confident and cheerful*. Her hair is dyed a pale pink colour, and she is wearing very trendy* clothes. Just at that moment, John comes back with his coffee. He nods* at Layla without speaking, and pushes past her to get through the doorway.

Layla raises* her eyebrows at you. 'See you later,' she says, and then she leaves.

Chapter 2

Section 23

There are also two emails from Karen. You open the first one.

Section 24

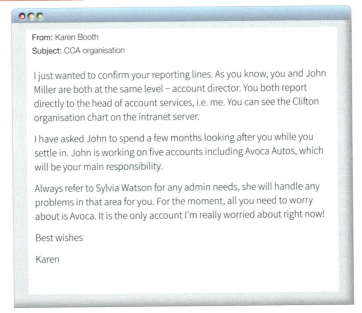

To check the organisation chart on the intranet server go to page 185. You open Karen's second email.

17

Chapter 2

25 Section 25

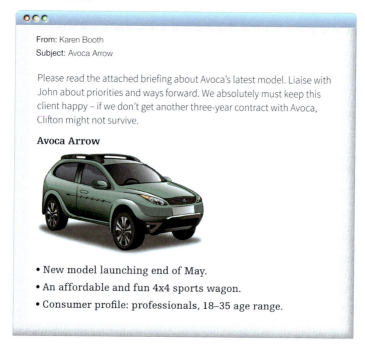

From: Karen Booth
Subject: Avoca Arrow

Please read the attached briefing about Avoca's latest model. Liaise with John about priorities and ways forward. We absolutely must keep this client happy – if we don't get another three-year contract with Avoca, Clifton might not survive.

Avoca Arrow

- New model launching end of May.
- An affordable and fun 4x4 sports wagon.
- Consumer profile: professionals, 18–35 age range.

You read a few more pages about the Avoca Arrow. Then you decide to listen to your voicemails. You press 'play' on the phone on your desk and listen. It is John Miller.

'It's me, John. Sorry about yesterday, it was a really stressful day! Hopefully things will be calmer now I have you as an assistant*. I just wanted to say that I'm going to be a bit late into work today. A personal matter. Let's meet at 10.30 and I can go through a few things with you. Bye for now!'

'Me? John's assistant?' you think. 'That's not what Karen's email says.'

26 Section 26

You go into the office that you share* with John Miller. You are sharing the office with John because he is going to teach you about account management. You know lots about the auto industry*, but you need to learn how to manage clients* and to do things from the ad agency's point

Chapter 2

of view. You will be working with John on Avoca Autos and a few other accounts.

You sit down at your desk and drop your bag on the floor. It is very quiet in the office. All you can hear is the hum* of the air con. You take your laptop* out of your bag and log on. You have some new email messages waiting for you. There are also some voicemail messages on your phone. You open an email message from HR* first.

▶ section 23

Section 27

John sits down at his desk. 'So, what was all that about?' he asks.

'Nothing. Layla was introducing herself. Apparently she's on the Avoca account.'

'Apparently she is,' he says quietly. 'Right! The Avoca Arrow.' He spends five minutes telling you things you have just read.

'John, can I stop you there?' you ask politely. 'I've had a chance to read all about the car this morning. I think I know who this new model* is aimed* at because the intended customers were very similar at my old company. But what do *they* think of the Arrow? Have you done any work with the target* market – you know, focus groups or surveys* – to see what their reaction is?'

'Ha!' laughs John. 'You don't want to worry about all that research*. You just need to get to know the product. We've got one on loan* from Avoca. It's just arrived. It's a great car to drive, so I'm told – really powerful. They've lent* us the V8 model. Take it for a drive. Get a feel for it. Take a few passengers with you and get some feedback* from them.'

19

Chapter 2

'Have you been in it yet?
'No, not yet.'

Who do you invite to try out the car with you?

1 John Miller ▶ section 28

2 Layla Evans ▶ section 37

3 Sylvia Watson ▶ section 35

28 Section 28

In the car park, the Avoca Arrow looks impressive. 'A boy racer's car,' you say.

'Absolutely,' says John. He gives you the key fob. 'You can drive.'

You get in and the smell of the new leather seats fills your nose. It certainly has a very luxurious interior. You are impressed*. The car has a keyless ignition system, so you press a button and the engine starts. The V8 engine makes a low, satisfying sound.

'Cool*. Where shall we go?' you ask.

'Head north, let's go over the Harbour* Bridge to the city centre,' says John.

You drive out of the car park and head north along Pittwater Road.

29 Section 29

The roads are quiet and the journey into central Sydney is quick. The Avoca Arrow is a great car to drive because it has a powerful engine. 'I love Sydney Harbour Bridge, don't you?' you ask.

John is holding onto the handle above his door. 'I like the bridge, but not your driving!' he says, angrily.

'What's wrong? Am I going too fast? Are you feeling sick?'

'No, but you haven't got a clue how to drive! You're driving in two lanes* at the moment – why can't you choose one or the other? And you never look or indicate before you change lanes. It's dangerous!'

'Oh, I'm sorry. Why don't you drive instead?'

'No, thanks.'

'I insist! It's great fun.'

Chapter 2

'Actually, I can't drive at the moment. I've lost my licence*.'
'Why?'
'Speeding*.'

You take John back to the office. On the way back, John mentions Sylvia. 'You shouldn't listen to everything Sylvia says. She's very sweet, of course, but she does get facts and fantasy a bit confused*, you know.'

You want to drive the car more so you take a second test drive.

Section 30

'Ha, ha!' laughs Layla when she sees the car. 'I knew it would look like this. It's like something from *Need for Speed*. Why are cars so macho these days?'

'I know what you mean,' you say. 'But it's nice inside.' You both get in.

'Hmm. That smell!'

'It's the leather seats,' you explain. You talk about the engine and a few other technical aspects of the car.

'Sorry to interrupt you,' Layla says, 'but how is it for connectivity?'

'Connect what?' you ask.

'Connectivity. How can I play my music?'

You look at the instrument panel. You find the radio and CD player, but there is no socket to connect a phone or MP3 player to the stereo. You can't connect to the system using Bluetooth either.

'It gets a low score for tech,' says Layla. 'I mean, come on, who uses CDs nowadays? A car like this should have Bluetooth or at least an input for music.' You hadn't noticed this, but she is right.

Section 31

You drive out of the car park and head south along Pittwater Road to Manly Beach. 'Let's go up to North Head,' says Layla. 'I want to go faster!' North Head is an area of woodland surrounded by cliffs that go down to

21

Chapter 2

the sea. It is quiet and there are kangaroos up there. You take a steep road out of Manly and then turn onto an old road towards North Head.

You accelerate* and the car flies over the rough road. Then you hear a very loud scream. 'Whoo!' Layla laughs. 'This is brilliant. I love hard suspension. You can really feel the wheels on the road. Can I drive?'

'Are you insured*?'

'Who cares?'

'Well ... OK.' You swap* seats and Layla drives. You get to a junction where you can go either left or right. To the left, the road loops around to a viewing area where tourists are taking photos of the harbour*. Layla turns right. She is driving really fast now. Suddenly, you see a man ahead waving* both arms.

'Ha! An Avoca fan!' says Layla.

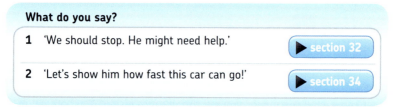

32 Section 32

Layla brakes* and the car stops very quickly. 'Hi,' she says to the man. 'What's up?'

'There's a flood* across the road. It doesn't look dangerous, but it's actually two metres deep. You can't go on. Turn back, we're going to close the road.'

'A flood?' you ask. 'But it's really dry today.'

'Some water pipes have broken,' the man replies.

'OK, thanks for the warning*,' says Layla and you drive back to work. You talk about the car and you agree that you are both very impressed. The body shape isn't to your taste, but the driving experience is fantastic.

Just as you are parking in the Clifton car park, Layla says, 'A word of warning. John might not be as helpful as he seems. I'm not going to say any more, but you should be careful with him. I don't really trust him.'

'Really?' you say. 'I'll remember that. Thanks, Layla.'

Chapter 2

Section 33

When you get back to your office, the telephone rings. 'Hello?'

'Hi,' Karen says. 'I'm at Melbourne airport. I can't talk for long, but I wanted to check how your day went.'

'Oh, right. Great, thank you. I've read all about the Arrow and I've taken it for a test drive. I think I know what our customers will like about the car.'

'Really? That was quick! Have you read the results of the surveys and the focus groups?'

'No, I haven't. Should I?'

'Of course!' shouts Karen. 'We've paid thousands of dollars for that research*. Without that information, how can we tell Avoca what their customers think of the product? And how can our creative teams work out how to sell the car if they don't know what the customers like? It's essential*! Get it from John.'

John didn't tell you the research was important. In fact, he advised you to forget about it. 'Right,' you say. 'I'll get the information from John. Thanks, Karen.'

Section 34

Layla brakes* for a sharp corner then goes faster again along the straight road. 'Watch out!' you shout. 'There's water across the road!'

'Brilliant! This should be fun,' says Layla. She aims the car for the middle of the water in the road and drives even faster. Water sprays everywhere, but suddenly the car slows down, and then it stops completely. The engine stops. You look at each other and then at the road, but there is no road. The car is floating. Quickly, you undo the seat belts and climb out of the windows. The water is deep and you have to swim to the edge.

The man arrives, running. 'I tried to tell you,' he says. 'There's a flood*. We're going to close the road.'

'Oh, no,' you say. 'Look at the car!' The car is sinking under the water.

'Look at my clothes and hair!' screams Layla.

'I don't believe it! I have to call work.' You get out your phone, but it is wet and it doesn't work.

Chapter 2

35 Section 35

You and Sylvia get into the car. You press a button and the engine starts. 'How did you do that?' asks Sylvia.

'Do what?' you ask.

'Start the car.'

'The car has a keyless ignition system.'

'Very modern!'

'I think it's quite typical in modern cars,' you say. 'All the ones in my old company had them.' You drive out of the car park and head south along Pittwater Road and down to Manly Beach. It is a perfect spring day, with a bright blue sky. The car windows are open and you can smell the sea air.

36 Section 36

'I wanted to tell you a bit more about John,' Sylvia says.

'Really? It seems a bit unprofessional. He is my colleague* after all,' you reply.

'Nonsense*! You're working with him, so it's only fair that you know about his reputation.'

'Go on then.'

'I'm not sure why, but he's made a lot of bad decisions recently. I don't think Karen trusts him and there's a danger he could lose the Avoca contract. Just be careful and make your own decisions about things. That's why Karen hired* you. And remember, he might not be completely honest. He's lied before.'

'That's all very interesting. So, what do you think?' you ask.

'Well, I agree with Karen …'

'No, I mean what do you think about the car?'

'Oh. Nice. Comfortable,' she says. 'I wouldn't want one for myself, of course, but for someone younger like you, it seems like a good car.' Sylvia tells you more about her own life. 'I get to work at about 7.30 every day so I can finish early and pick my son up from school at 4.00 p.m.'

You drive slowly, stopping for people who run across the road to the beach. You pass a busy square with ice cream and surf shops. Sylvia asks you to stop so she can buy something, but she doesn't have an opinion about the car – she is in the wrong age group to be an Arrow customer.

Chapter 2

You drive back to the Clifton offices and decide to take Layla out for a test drive instead.

 section 30

Section 37

⭐ You win 1 bonus point. Mark the scorecard on page 186.
Good choice! Layla fits the target* profile for the Avoca Arrow. She is in the right age group and she has a professional career*. It was a good idea to invite Layla.

 section 30

Section 38

You walk back to the office with Layla, but you don't speak very much. The sun is hot and it dries your clothes. When you eventually* get back to the Clifton offices, you look and feel terrible*. Karen is waiting in reception. She looks very serious. 'What happened to you?' she asks.

'We had a little accident,' you say. You explain what happened with the Avoca Arrow.

Karen looks very angry. 'Who was driving?' she asks.

You remember that Layla isn't insured to drive. 'I was,' you say eventually, 'but I'm sure my insurance* will cover it. Tomorrow, I'll—'

'No,' Karen interrupts you. 'Don't come in tomorrow. In fact, don't come back again. I'm sorry, but you'll have to leave the company.'

Your career* in advertising only lasted 2 days!

Go back to the start of the chapter and try again.   section 20

25

Chapter 3

39 Section 39

Eva Campano is talking loudly. Eva is the creative director at Clifton Creative Agency, so she is in charge of the content of the company's advertising campaigns*. The copywriters* and art directors report to her and she has to approve* all their slogans* and images. Eva is presenting her team's main idea for the Avoca Arrow campaign. You are sitting with John and Layla, listening.

'This is it!' Eva says. As she speaks, her jewellery* clicks together. 'This is great. There's a family – a typical suburban* family. It's the middle of the afternoon and mum's gardening while dad's watching TV. Their son is about six years old. Either he's bored or he wants to help his parents by doing the shopping. Either way, he decides to take out his dad's car – an Avoca Arrow. He's too short to reach the pedals*, so he uses a brick, just like in this picture. Then he drives to the shops. The boy has a brilliant time, and the slogan is "The Avoca Arrow – so easy to drive, it's child's play." What do you think? Do you see what I mean?' Eva stares at you. You are not sure what to say, so you say nothing.

Two weeks have passed since you started at Clifton and this is your first big meeting with the creative team. You have read all the reports and surveys*, and you have written a brief* for the creative team. They are now sharing their ideas with you, but you are worried that they haven't understood your brief.

26

Chapter 3

Section 40

'Very interesting,' you say. 'Of course, we're preparing for the first meeting with the client* so we need several ideas to present to them. I wonder if you could show us any other ideas?'

'Certainly,' says Eva. 'But you must realise that none of the ideas are as good as this one. This idea is dynamite!'

John is sitting with his arms folded. He doesn't look impressed. 'Just show us your other ideas, Eva,' he says. 'We'll decide which ones to show the client.'

'That's what I'm afraid of!' Eva replies. 'OK, let's look at the others.'

Section 41

'I love it!' you say. 'It's funny, adventurous, brave and very original. What a cool* idea!'

Eva looks delighted*. She gives you a big smile. 'I'm so happy you like it,' she says. 'We really think it'll work. It could be a really memorable* ad.'

'Hang on*,' says John. 'Calm down everyone. Let's see the other ideas first. I mean, there might be some other "memorable ads" waiting for us.'

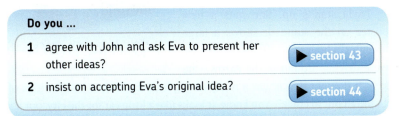

Chapter 3

42 Section 42

'I don't believe this,' you say. 'How can we possibly present this idea to a client?* You know that we're not allowed to show illegal acts in our ads. This is a six-year-old boy driving a car! It's unacceptable. Didn't you read the brief I gave you?'

Eva's face goes red. Layla also looks angry. John Miller gives a little smile.

'Your brief?' says Eva. 'That was the worst brief I've seen in twenty years in this business! It didn't have any useful information in it. We can't work without something to start from.'

'My brief was excellent,' you say. 'You're just not following my instructions.'

'My team has worked night and day on this project,' says Eva. 'You should show more respect for our hard work.'

> **What do you say?**
>
> 1 'All right, I'm sorry. Let's look at the other ideas that your team have come up with.'
>
> 2 'If I give you a brief, you should follow it. I know more about the car industry than anyone here.'

43 Section 43

'Right,' says Eva. 'So we spent a lot of time brainstorming* ideas about the Avoca Arrow. The best idea, as I say, is the "child's play" ad, but we have two more. One has the slogan, "A tough nut* to crack". Layla, talk us through this one.'

Layla stands up. She puts a new poster on the stand. It shows a large hammer* about to hit the car. 'When we were driving around in the Arrow,' she

says, 'I thought that it was a really strong little car. So we had the idea of "A tough nut to crack". You know, it looks like a little car for the city, but it's well built and it'll never break down. Even a hammer couldn't damage* it.'

'Nice,' says John.

'We've got one more idea,' says Eva. 'We wanted to emphasise* the environmental benefits* of the Avoca Arrow. It's made in a modern factory with little CO_2 pollution. It doesn't use as much fuel* as other 4x4s. Young people want to be "green" so it's the perfect car for them. Our slogan is "The green machine". One visual idea we're looking at is showing the car with trees and plants growing out of it, and lots of animals like rabbits and birds all around.'

'Uh-huh,' says John.

The meeting continues for another hour, but at the end there are just these three ideas left. John doesn't like the 'child's play' idea, but Eva insists that everyone thinks about it.

'OK, everyone,' says John, 'let's sleep on these ideas and we'll have a final meeting tomorrow. Then we'll decide which ideas to show to Avoca.'

Do you ...

1 compliment all of the ideas? ▶ section 56

2 compliment your favourite idea? ▶ section 49

Section 44

'I think this is the perfect campaign idea,' you say. 'Let's take it to the meeting with the client*.'

'We don't work like that,' says John. 'You don't understand the business. We always take several ideas to the client. Sometimes we present a few weak* ideas along with an idea that we really like. That way, the weak ideas make the good one look better.'

'I really want to show Avoca the ad with the kid in the car,' you repeat.

'I've told you,' says John, 'we need more suggestions. Eva please, show us the other plans from your department.'

You want to say something else, but John looks at you angrily so you decide to wait.

▶ section 43

Chapter 3

45 Section 45

Eva still looks angry.

'Don't worry,' says John. 'We have a very inexperienced account director here, someone who doesn't know how this business works yet. Let's see the other ideas. I'm keen* to see them. Show us anything you've got. You're only showing us your initial* ideas, after all.'

You feel annoyed*. John has embarrassed* you in front of your colleagues*. Fortunately, Eva seems happy now so she continues with the meeting.

46 Section 46

'Don't you tell me how to do my job,' says Eva, 'I've been the creative director here for ten years. You've been in the industry two weeks and suddenly you're an expert on everything.'

'I may be new to advertising, but I do understand the auto industry*,' you reply. 'You should listen to what I have to say.'

'I've already heard enough,' says Eva. Picking up her papers, she walks out of the room. She leaves only one thing on the desk – the brief that you wrote. Layla follows her, almost running to walk at the same speed.

'Now you've caused a real problem,' says John.

47 Section 47

That evening, you are at home when your phone rings. It is Karen, your boss. Although it is 9.00 at night, she gets straight down to business. 'I heard about the meeting today,' she says.

'I'm pleased that you've phoned me,' you say. 'We've got a bit of a problem with the creative team. I don't think they've followed the brief.'

'No,' Karen replies. 'The problem isn't them – it's you. The creative team is furious* with you and we don't have time to repair* the damage.'

'What do you mean?'

'Look,' says Karen, 'your management style doesn't fit with our company. The creative team are a bit like artists. You have to be careful about what you say to them. I'm taking you off the Avoca project, and … I don't want you to come into work tomorrow.' There is a pause.

Chapter 3

'Are you sacking* me?' you ask.

'I'm afraid so,' Karen replies.

You have lost your job. Your advertising career is over.

Go back to the start of the chapter and try again. section 39

Section 48

Your phone rings. It is someone from Avoca Autos.

'Hi, it's Hans Fischer's PA* here,' she says.

'Oh hello,' you say. 'I hope everything is OK for tomorrow's meeting.'

'Oh yes,' she replies. 'Hans wanted to know if he could bring Dagmar.'

'Er, yes, of course,' you say. 'I look forward to meeting them both tomorrow.'

 section 58

Section 49

You pick up your favourite design and tell everyone how much you love it. Eva and Layla are pleased, but John does not look comfortable.

'I think this is such a great idea,' you say.

'We don't want to make a final decision yet,' says John. 'We'll talk about it again tomorrow.'

'Yes, but this idea is fantastic,' you say.

You leave the meeting with John while the creative team stay behind to collect their papers and presentations.

When you get back to your office, John closes the door. 'What were you thinking?' he says. 'You don't have the right to make a decision like that now! We're choosing several ads to show to the client, not just one.'

'I'm sorry. I loved the ad and I just wanted to tell everyone.'

'Next time, wait,' says John. 'Anyway, remember, it's the client that makes the final decision. In the case of Avoca Autos, that means Hans Fischer. You'll meet him soon, and trust me, he's a difficult man to please.'

 section 50

31

Chapter 3

50 Section 50

That night, you decide to work outside on your balcony. It has been a hot day so it is nice to enjoy the cool evening air. Across the street, the lights are on in your neighbour's house and you can hear their radio. The adverts start and you listen to them carefully. Your life is changing. You never used to notice the ads, and now they are the thing that you listen to most.

Smiling, you turn on your laptop* and see you have a message from your old friend Pete Deng. You and Pete went to university together. Pete lives in the beautiful region of Gondwanaland, on the other side of the Australia. He works for the Gondwanaland Tourism Board.

'Hi, it's me. Sorry I haven't been in touch for a while. Things have been really busy at work recently. So anyway, how's your new job going? Oh, that reminds me. Guess* what! I found out* that your company does the advertising for the Gondwanaland Tourism Board. So, who knows? Maybe we'll be working together some time in the future. It'll be like university days all over again! Anyway, give me a call when you can, OK? Chat soon.'

You see that Pete is still online and you Skype him. 'Hey,' he says with a big smile. 'Did you get my message?'

'Yes, you reply. 'I've just listened to it. How are things with you?'

'Better now, but I had a crazy couple of weeks at work. And you? Tell me about the new job.'

Do you ...

1 say everything is OK and not mention the Avoca Autos project? ▶ section 51

2 tell Pete everything about the meeting with the creative team? ▶ section 57

Chapter 3

Section 51

'That's good news,' says Pete. 'Clifton has done some great advertising work for Gondwanaland. I'm pleased you're happy there.'

'Yeah,' you say, 'I hope I'll get to work on a project for you someday. What's the weather like over there?'

'It's spectacular*,' says Pete. 'Gondwanaland is like paradise. Clear blue skies, crystal clear water and beaches with sand as white as sugar. Ask your company to send you out here. You'll love it!'

You and Pete talk a bit longer about life and other friends before the call ends. You feel a lot better after talking to your old friend again.

Section 52

As the others go out of the meeting room, Eva walks towards you. 'I had some doubts* at first,' she says, 'but now I'm glad* you're working here.'

'Thanks,' you say.

'I think it's very important that the creative team and the account directors have a similar vision, don't you?'

'Yes, I suppose so.'

'To be honest with you, John just doesn't understand what we're trying to do, but you're different. I think we'll be able to make some fantastic ads together.' Her eyes light up, 'Maybe even win some awards!'

'Maybe we will,' you say, smiling.

'Look, if have any problems with John, or anything, just ring me – my extension is 060.'

Write down Eva's extension in the Contacts section on page 186.

You go back to your desk and carry on* working.

Section 53

The next day you have the second meeting about the Avoca Arrow campaign. This time Layla doesn't come, so it is just you, John and Eva. Sylvia is there to take the minutes*. You discuss the ideas for an hour.

Eventually*, John asks everyone to make a final decision. 'OK, we need to choose which ideas to present to Avoca Autos at our first meeting with them next week. So far, we have three ideas. First, "A tough nut to

33

Chapter 3

crack". We all agree that's interesting. We also have the idea of "The green machine". Are we all happy with both of these?'

'Yes,' you say.

'Absolutely,' Eva agrees.

'Fine,' says John. Then he sighs. 'Now we have this third idea. The kid in the car with the slogan, "So easy to drive, it's child's play". Personally, I feel that this idea is not one that we can present to the client. I vote *no*.'

'I'm afraid I disagree,' says Eva. 'This is for an initial ideas meeting, and we should be ambitious. I vote *yes*.'

'So,' says John, 'that's one vote for the idea and one vote against it. The final decision is yours. Do we present "It's child's play" to the client?'

54 Section 54

John looks shocked. 'Are you sure?' he asks.

'Excellent!' Eva says. 'Finally, we have an imaginative account director!'

'I can imagine a lot of things that will happen if we show this idea to Hans,' says John.

'I think it's really original,' you say. 'It's just an initial meeting. It's a good opportunity to present some fun and interesting ideas.'

'Accept it, John,' says Eva. 'The vote is two to one, so we're presenting all three ideas, including the child's play ad.'

'Fine, but Sylvia, please note in the minutes that I voted against the idea,' says John.

55 Section 55

'That's final, then,' says John. 'Two votes to one. We reject* "it's child's play" and we present the two other ideas to Avoca.'

'Typical,' says Eva. 'You account directors are all the same. You're not interested in new ideas. You just want the same old thing.'

34

Chapter 3

'We listened to all your ideas, but we voted against that one,' says John. 'That's fair, isn't it?'

'You're all so conservative!' says Eva. 'Well, I've said everything I have to say. You've made your decision and I'll have to accept it.'

'I'm sorry,' you say.

'I'm not,' says John.

The meeting comes to an end. You go back to your desk and carry on* working.

▶ section 48

Section 56

'I think your team has done a great job,' you say.

'I agree,' says John. 'There are lots of strong ideas here.'

'Well, let's see what we decide tomorrow,' says Eva. 'But thanks for your support*. The final ideas always look simple, but it takes a long time to get them right.'

'Right everyone, thank you very much,' says John. 'Let's end the meeting there for today. We'll meet again tomorrow.'

▶ section 50

Section 57

⭐ You win 1 bonus point. Mark the scorecard on page 186.

You tell Pete about the meeting today. He is an old friend and you trust him. You explain the creative team's initial* ideas and how you felt about them.

'Hm …' says Pete. 'Take my advice. Be very careful. In advertising agencies, the creative team often come up with crazy ideas. Sometimes they seem more interested in winning awards than producing ads that clients really want.'

'What are you saying?' you ask.

'I think the ad with the kid in the car is a bad idea,' he replies. 'Your client will hate it. It's obviously an attempt to shock people and win an advertising award. Avoca Autos won't like that ad if you present it to them.' This is very useful advice!

You and Pete talk a bit longer about life and other friends before the call ends. You feel a lot better after talking to your old friend again.

Chapter 4

58 Section 58

You feel nervous. You have butterflies* in your stomach. Your hands are sweating* even though the air con in your office is on full-power. You are nervous because you have your first big meeting today, and you have to pitch* your ideas. This is why you were hired* to work at Clifton Creative Agency – you have to impress Hans Fischer and keep the Avoca Autos account.

John Miller has told you a little about Hans, but you know nothing about Dagmar, his colleague*. What is her role and what is she like? Hans and Dagmar were due to meet you at 10.30 am. It is now 11.13 and they still have not arrived. Did you tell Hans the wrong date or time for the meeting? Suddenly, your phone rings. You jump in your seat. 'I have Hans Fischer here in reception for you.'

You look at John, but he is talking on the phone. You rush* out of your office, swipe* your security card and go through the doors into reception. You are horrified* – a small dog is attacking a smartly-dressed man and woman who are sitting on the sofa. You think that these are your clients, Hans and Dagmar. The dog is barking* a lot, though it isn't actually biting anyone. The noise of the barking is terrible* in the small reception area.

A huge* man with blond hair is holding the dog's lead and shouting something at the dog.

▶ section 59

Chapter 4

Section 59

'She is so ... disobedient*!' says the blond man with a foreign accent. Eventually*, he pulls the dog back.

You look at your clients and hold up your hands in disbelief. 'I do apologise* about that.' You shake hands with them. 'Hi. You must be Hans Fischer and Dagmar. I'm your new account director. I'm working with John Miller on the Arrow account.'

'I don't know who John Miller is, mate*. I'm Adam, we're here about the cleaning contract* for the offices.' says the man.

You look at the woman. 'You aren't Dagmar, then?'

'No. I'm Carrie. Cleaning services manager. How are you?'

'Fine, thanks. Listen, I've got you confused* with someone else, I'm afraid.'

You look at the receptionist. 'Where is Mr Fischer?' you ask her.

Before she can answer, the dog starts barking again. 'Shh! *Es ist ja gut*!' the blond man shouts at the dog. You look around to see what the matter is. 'You!' the big man shouts, pointing* his finger at you.

Do you ...

1 wait to hear what the man wants to say? ▶ section 61

2 tell the man with the dog to leave? ▶ section 68

Section 60

Suddenly there is a sound of barking outside. 'I'll go,' you say. 'It must be Dagmar.' You go outside. A man is jogging* on the beach. Dagmar is running in a circle around his feet, barking at him. He stops running and stands with his arms held high.

You run over. 'I'm so sorry! Let me take this naughty* dog away!'

'You aren't allowed to have dogs on the beach!'

'Oh, really? Listen, I know whose dog it is. I'll take it back to him and tell him not to let it on the beach again.'

'Thanks, mate. I was going to call the police.'

You lead Dagmar back to the meeting room. 'Oh, my little Dagmar, where have you been?' asks Hans.

37

Chapter 4

You are out of breath and very hot. 'She ... she ... was just playing! But dogs aren't allowed on the beach so I've brought her inside. I'll get her a bowl of water.'

 section 69

61 Section 61

The large blond man takes a deep breath. 'My name is Fischer. Hans Fischer,' he says with a German accent. 'I do apologise for my dog's behaviour. She gets very excited when she meets new people.'

'Oh! I'm very pleased to meet you, Mr Fischer. Welcome to Clifton.'

You offer Hans your right hand. He looks at it, then puts the dog's lead into his left hand and shakes your hand. 'I am pleased to meet you too. John Miller has told me about you.'

'Oh. Good,' you say.

Hans looks at the young couple and says, 'Young man, lady, I must apologise. My dog, she loves strong smells.'

'No worries mate,' says the man. 'I've got five dogs of my own at home.'

62 Section 62

'So, Mr Fischer ...'

'Call me Hans.'

'So, Hans, shall we wait for Dagmar? Will she be long?'

Hans looks down at the dog. It is chewing* the end of your shoe. You shake your foot and it growls*. 'This,' he says, pointing at the dog, 'is Dagmar. She comes everywhere with me.'

John Miller never mentioned that Dagmar was a dog! Hans picks her up in his enormous* hands and holds her in his arms. Dagmar's face is almost the same height as yours and she growls at you.

'Shall we?' asks Hans, gesturing* towards the doors.

38

Chapter 4

'Of course,' you say again, swiping* your security card and opening the door for Hans.

Hans walks confidently into the agency boardroom*. 'So?' he asks, cheerfully.

'So,' you say. 'The time is ... nearly 11.30. We have a meeting with the creative team ... now, in fact, but it's not here, it's in Manly, by the beach. Why don't I drive you to the venue* and we can chat on the way?'

Section 63

You, John and Hans are walking towards the Avoca Arrow in the car park. 'Nice car!' Hans jokes.

John opens a rear door and Hans and Dagmar get into the car. 'You don't drive, John?' Hans asks.

'Not this time. I'll let our new account director drive.'

You drive out onto Pittwater Road. It is very sunny and the road is empty. Soon, you arrive at Shelly Beach. It is a perfect horseshoe shape and not very wide. It feels private. You could almost believe you were on a tropical island a thousand kilometres from the busy city. You park and walk down to the shore. Dagmar chases* a seagull* into the sea. You go towards the only building on the small beach, a large brick building that used to be for fishing boats, but has been converted into a gallery for fashionable artists.

Section 64

'So, Mr Fischer ...'

'Call me Hans.'

'So, Hans, how was your journey*?'

'I am afraid I was delayed. Nothing is efficient here compared with Germany, but at least I had Dagmar with me.' You look around expecting* to see his female colleague. Hans kneels* and pats the dog's head. It starts to chew* the end of your shoe. You don't think you should stop it. You realise that Dagmar must be the dog!

'What a sweet little dog. How long have you had Dagmar?'

'You shouldn't ask a lady her age, you should know that.'

'Of course.'

Chapter 4

Hans takes Dagmar in his enormous* hands and stands up. Dagmar's face is almost the same height as yours and she growls* at you.

'We have a meeting with the creative team,' you say. 'It's not here though. It's in Manly, by the beach. Why don't I drive you to the venue* and we can chat on the way?'

65 Section 65

You go inside the old building and find the meeting room you hired for today's meeting. You see that your colleagues* Eva and Layla have arrived before you. They introduce themselves. 'Hello, Hans. I'm Eva Campano, the creative director on the Arrow campaign. This is Layla Evans. She's our copywriter*.'

'Nice to meet you, Mr Fischer,' says Layla.

'You too, Layla. So, what are we doing today? No lunch?' asks Hans.

'Well, we thought we'd start with the meeting,' laughs John. 'Then lunch! What we really want from today is to agree on an SMP for the Arrow.'

'You people love your acronyms*!' laughs Hans.

'SMP?' you ask.

'Yes. A Single Minded Proposition. So the SMP for Nike is "Just do it", for example,' says John.

'OK. So an SMP is like a Unique Selling Point?'

'Well, similar to a USP,' agrees John. 'The purpose of today's meeting is to share* some SMPs that we have developed for the Arrow. We want to agree on the best SMP with you, then we can develop some advertising campaigns* based on it.'

'I've written a draft brief* for the creative team, with John's help,' you explain. 'The brief gives them all the information about the product and the potential customers for the car. After today, we'll have an SMP that Clifton and Avoca agree is the best message. I'll update* the brief. Then the creative team can design some adverts to fit the SMP.'

'Great.' says Hans. 'Just do it!' He roars* with laughter.

40

Chapter 4

Section 66

You start the meeting. 'The first SMP is "The Avoca Arrow – the green machine". The idea is that the car is economical on fuel* and good for the environment – ideal for young people's budgets* and their concerns* about the environment.'

'Green, green, green! Everything these days is *green*. We want something more original than that.'

'We like "the green machine",' says Layla.

'Well, I don't!' says Hans. 'No good. Next?'

'OK,' says Eva. She looks upset. 'The next SMP is "The Avoca Arrow – a tough nut*". So we might have a line in a TV ad that uses the expression "a tough nut to crack". It's based on the idea that it's a small but a very strong, tough little car.'

'What is this "nut" phrase? Does "a tough nut to crack" have some sort of special meaning?'

'Yes, I guess so,' you say. 'If something is a tough nut to crack, it means that whatever you do to this thing – this nut or this car – nothing can break it. Eva – the artwork?'

'Here,' she says. 'This can change, of course, it's just a very initial* idea for the kind of image that could accompany the SMP "a tough nut to crack". Er ...'

'Yes! I like this!' shouts Hans, and he bangs a big fist on the table, smiling.

Eva smiles at you.

Section 67

Look at the Contacts section on page 186.

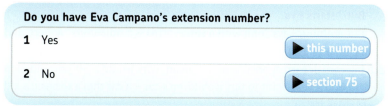

Chapter 4

Section 68

'You can't bring a dog in here!' you shout. 'This is an advertising agency! We have important customers coming in and out.'

'What do you mean?' the man complains*. 'I have a meeting here!'

'Really?' you say. 'Who with?'

The man says your name. You are very surprised. Then you realise your mistake*, 'Oh,' you say. 'Are you Hans Fischer?'

'Of course I am! I asked if I could bring Dagmar, my dog, and you said "yes". Now you shout at me and insult me in this way. I ... I don't know what to say.' The man is red-faced and angry. He turns around and walks out of the main door. Dagmar the dog looks back at you and then the door closes behind them.

Hans does not come back to the office. You have just lost one of Clifton's most important clients*.

Go back to the start of the chapter and try again.

Section 69

Just then Karen Booth enters the room. 'Hello, I didn't realise you were coming,' Eva says.

'I'm here for lunch with my old friend Hans,' Karen says. 'Don't let me stop you. Carry on*, please!'

Eva smiles at you again. 'OK. This is the best of the three ideas, I think,' she says. 'The SMP is "So easy to drive, it's child's play". The TV ad could be something like this – a family scene in a normal household ...' She describes the ad with the six-year-old boy who drives the family car. Finally, she says, 'What do you think? It's great, isn't it?'

'What's this?' asks Hans. 'Is this a joke or something?'

'But–' starts Eva.

'But nothing,' says John with a smile. 'This is a ridiculous* advert, and it's illegal too! The government bans* any adverts which show under-17s driving cars. It's irresponsible and, I mean, why would a 30-year-old man on $50,000 a year want to buy a children's car – a car that's so basic a kid could drive it?'

'I completely agree,' says Karen. 'I can't believe you thought this was

Chapter 4

a good idea.'

'I tried to stop them,' says John. You feel your cheeks going red. John gets a dog biscuit out of his pocket and gives it to Dagmar. She eats it happily and Hans smiles again.

'I hope some of the other ideas were interesting, Hans?' asks Karen.
'You're a tough nut to crack!'
'What do you mean?' replies Karen. She looks worried and a bit offended.
'You're a tough nut to crack. It's the SMP I want for the Arrow.'
'The idea that Hans liked best was "It's a tough nut to crack",' you explain.
'Oh, I see. Very nice! So, Hans, are you happy with that slogan*?'
'Very happy,' he says.
'OK,' says Karen, 'shall we go outside, if the meeting's finished?'

Section 70

A speedboat arrives at the shore. 'Great! Lunch,' says Karen. 'Hans, this is the speedboat to take us across to Watson's Bay. We're going to Doyles restaurant. They have the best fish in Sydney!'

'Wow,' you say.
'Great!' says Layla.

Karen looks at the team and shakes her head. 'It's lunch for two, I'm afraid. Please take Dagmar back to the agency and look after her. We'll see you later. Let's go, Hans!'

Chapter 4

Section 71

Back at the office, you and the creative team celebrate the successful meeting. John doesn't join you, he is busy. At 4.30, you are updating your documents to create a final Avoca Arrow brief for the creative team. Suddenly, you hear an unusual sound. It sounds like a jingle – a song for an ad.

'It's a tough, tough, tough nut to crack. It's a tough, tough, tough nut to crack!'

It is singing. Then you recognise* the phrase, 'It's a tough nut to crack', followed by laughter. Dagmar, who is on the floor next to your desk, suddenly looks up and wags her tail. It is Hans.

'*You* are a tough nut!' he laughs.

'No, *you* are a tough nut!' replies Karen.

Sylvia gets them some coffees and they go to the boardroom.

▶ section 78

Section 72

'This is ridiculous!' you say. 'I'm here now. Why can't I just take the dog?'

'Rules are rules,' the ranger says.

What do you say?

1. 'The dog's owner is in that building over there. He's an important client of mine.' ▶ section 77

2. 'Why don't I just pay you $100 cash, then we can both forget about this situation?' ▶ section 76

Section 73

'Then we're going to take it to the council dog home. Perhaps its owner* will claim* it. Otherwise …' The ranger makes a sign with his hand across his throat.

'No!'

'What?'

'You can't do that!'

'It's the law,' says the ranger. He points to a sign.

Dogs are allowed on a lead under the effective control of a competent person. They are never allowed off the lead on beaches.

44

Chapter 4

'Dogs like this have to go to the council dog home. If the owner comes and pays the fine*, they can collect the dog.'

Section 74

'You think you understand cars!' shouts Hans. 'But you don't understand Avoca. Perhaps John can handle my account, like in the past?'

'Yes, of course,' Karen looks at you. 'Would you mind leaving us now?' she asks.

Later, Karen Booth tells you that you are no longer working on Avoca. Without the Avoca account, you have no projects of your own. You have to help John with his other accounts. He treats you like an assistant*.

After six weeks, you decide to resign* and leave Clifton Creative Agency.

Go back to the start of the chapter and try again.

Section 75

There is a sound of barking outside. 'I'll go,' you say. 'It must be Dagmar.' As you go outside you see Karen Booth walking towards the building. You wave at her and then you see three men are chasing Dagmar on the beach. They are wearing grey uniforms and caps. On the back of their jackets it says 'Council Ranger'. You run after them, but just before you reach them, one of the rangers jumps on Dagmar and catches her.

'What's going on? Leave that dog alone!' you shout.

'Is this your dog?' one of them asks.

45

Chapter 4

76 **Section 76**

That was a very bad idea. You can't bribe* a public official with cash*! The ranger calls the police. While you are apologising* to the police, Hans Fischer and your colleagues come out to see what is happening. You are in big trouble.

Later, after the meeting, Karen calls you. 'When I gave you this job, I thought you were an honest, careful professional. I now see that I've made a mistake*.'

'I was trying to save Dagmar and our contract* with Avoca!' you explain.

'You don't have to worry about that anymore,' says Karen. 'John will handle the Avoca contract on his own from now on. I'm sorry, but you must see that it's impossible to work with you again after this.'

You have been sacked*! You now have a criminal record as well.

Go back to the start of the chapter and try again.

77 **Section 77**

⭐ You win 1 bonus point. Mark the scorecard on page 186.
'So?' asks the man.

'I'm here on business and my client* brought his dog along. This is her – Dagmar. This client is really important to us and I don't want any trouble or I could lose my job. I'll pay the fine* now if you want. But please don't take poor Dagmar to the dog home.'

The ranger looks at you. 'Alright, I believe you,' he says. 'Look, it's my birthday today and I'm feeling generous. If you take the dog back now, we won't say anything more about it. But next time you're on my beach, make sure the dog is on a lead!'

'Oh, thank you! Thank you!' you say.

Good choice. Hans doesn't know that Dagmar was in trouble. Relieved*, you walk back along Shelly Beach with Dagmar. Hans Fischer and your colleagues are waiting for you outside the building.

'There they are!' shouts Layla.

Hans runs and kneels* in front of Dagmar. He tickles her ears and looks into her face. 'Oh, Dagmar! My little Dagmar! Where have you been? What happened to you, Dagmar?'

46

Chapter 4

'She ran away,' you explain. 'I saw her running along that road, and so I chased* her. She ran really fast, but eventually* she stopped and I caught her.'

'You're amazing. Thank you so much. I don't know what I would do without my little Dagmar.'

You smile and say, 'You're welcome, Mr Fischer …'

'Hans, please!' he insists.

'You're welcome, Hans. To be honest, I did it for Dagmar. She is such a lovely little dog.'

'She is,' Hans agrees. 'Thank you again.'

Section 78

Five minutes later, Sylvia calls. 'Can you and John come and join Hans and Karen, please?'

You go to the boardroom*. 'Was lunch good?' you ask.

'Yes, very good, thank you. Doyles – you should go there some time.'

'Listen,' says Karen. 'We've made an important decision. We're going to change the name of the Avoca Arrow.'

'What?' you and John say together.

'Yes,' says Hans. 'The name "Arrow" doesn't really work with the "tough nut" SMP. But try this: "The Avoca Acorn – a tough nut to crack!" Now that's brilliant. Do you get it? Nut – acorn.' He shows you a serviette from the restaurant with a sketch on it.

'We get it,' says John. He looks at you nervously. You know a lot about car names from your last job. 'Acorn' is a terrible* name for a car!

'What do you think about the new name?' Hans asks.

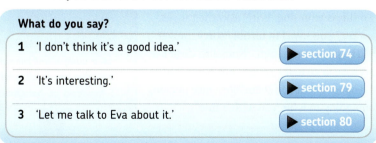

Chapter 4

Section 79

Good answer. You avoided* an argument*. The next day, Karen can't remember the conversation about the Avoca 'Acorn'. The car is still called the Avoca Arrow! You are very relieved*.

Section 80

That was a sensible answer. You tell Eva. She closes her eyes and shakes* her head. The next day, Karen has changed her mind* about the Avoca 'Acorn'. The car is still called the Avoca Arrow! Everyone on the team is happy again.

Section 81

You run back to the meeting room. 'Hans! It's Dagmar. The council rangers have taken her to the council dog home!'

'What? My Dagmar? How could this happen? This is terrible. The meeting is over. Where is the council dog home?' He rushes* outside, but the council rangers have gone. You see their van driving away. 'You have lost my dog,' says Hans angrily. He immediately calls a taxi and jumps inside.

Your colleagues come outside and look at you. You explain the situation. Very quietly, John says, 'You've lost Dagmar, and you've lost the Avoca contract too. Hans will never renew* the contract after this.'

One week later Karen tells you that Avoca have left Clifton.

Go back to the start of the chapter and try again.

Section 82

'So this is your dog, is it?' asks the ranger.

'Yes,' you say. 'I'm terribly sorry, ranger.'

He points at a sign. 'Normally, dogs like this have to go to the council dog home. But as it's your dog and you seem like a nice person, I am going to issue you with a fine*.'

> Dogs are allowed on a lead under the effective control of a competent person. They are never allowed off the lead on beaches.

48

Chapter 4

'Oh, really? A fine? How much?'

'It's $200.'

You decide to pay the fine with your own money. It is a lot, but you don't want anything to go wrong with the meeting. The ranger gives you a receipt and hands the dog to you. You put Dagmar on her lead and go back to the building. Everyone is waiting for you outside.

49

Chapter 5

83 Section 83

Everything is going well at Clifton. You now have an SMP for your campaign*, 'The Avoca Arrow – a tough nut* to crack'. The creative team is working on final ideas for the TV campaign for your next meeting with Hans Fischer. It is a quiet day and you are alone in your office. John Miller is on holiday this week and Karen Booth, your line manager*, has meetings out of town. You are at your desk checking Facebook when suddenly the door opens. You close the program quickly. Fortunately, it is just Sylvia, the office manager.

'Sorry. Do you have a minute?' she asks.

'Of course, Sylvia, come in,' you say. 'What's the problem?'

'I've just had Hans on the phone,' she says.

'Oh. Is anything wrong?'

'Not exactly, he just asked us for a little favour*.'

'A favour? What does he want?'

'Well, last year, we invited all our customers to a summer party. At the party, we had these huge* signs with all our clients'* names spelt* out in two-metre foam letters. Hans was at the party and apparently he thought the letters were a brilliant idea because now, he's asking if we can make some similar letters for his daughter's eighteenth birthday party. He wants to spell out her name – Catherine.'

'Two-metre high letters! How are we going to do that? We're too busy!'

Chapter 5

'I'm sorry, but I've already said yes,' says Sylvia. 'I thought we had to keep Avoca happy.'

'Oh no,' you say, 'that's all we need!'

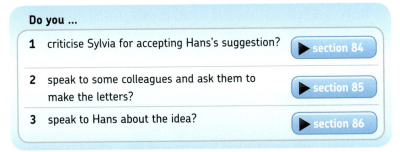

Do you ...

1. criticise Sylvia for accepting Hans's suggestion? ▶ section 84
2. speak to some colleagues and ask them to make the letters? ▶ section 85
3. speak to Hans about the idea? ▶ section 86

Section 84

'What were you thinking, Sylvia?' you ask. 'This means more work for all of us. Everyone's already working night and day on this project!'

Sylvia looks upset. 'It all happened so fast. You know what Hans is like. It's impossible to say "no" to him. I'm sorry ... I didn't think.'

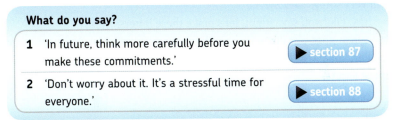

What do you say?

1. 'In future, think more carefully before you make these commitments.' ▶ section 87
2. 'Don't worry about it. It's a stressful time for everyone.' ▶ section 88

Section 85

You are not sure who can make the letters for you. You will need to ask a colleague to help you.

Do you ...

1. call Karen Booth, your manager? ▶ section 91
2. call Eva Campano, the creative director? ▶ section 92
3. call Layla Evans, your copywriter? ▶ section 93

Chapter 5

86 Section 86

You call Avoca Autos and ask to speak to Hans. 'Hello!' he laughs. 'You've been speaking to Sylvia, I think!'

'That's right,' you say. 'She told me about your plan for the letters.'

'You know, I really appreciate* this. My daughter will be so pleased. I wanted to arrange these letters for her birthday party and I didn't know how to do it.'

What do you say?

1 'I'm afraid there's a problem. We won't be able to make the letters on time. We're all too busy.' ▶ section 89

2 'We're happy to help. Could I just check the details with you?' ▶ section 98

87 Section 87

'I'm very sorry,' says Sylvia.

'OK, OK,' you say. 'Right, let's make these letters.'

Sylvia goes out of the room. She looks very unhappy. You feel sorry for her, but she did make a mistake*. Several people will have to work on these letters.

 section 85

88 Section 88

Sylvia looks very unhappy. 'Are you OK?' you ask. 'Sit down. What's wrong?'

'I'm sorry,' she says. 'I know it's not very professional, but I have a lot of problems at home at the moment.'

'Oh, no. Is it anything serious?'

'It's not serious ... it's not an illness or anything like that, I mean. It's my son, Jack. I'm bringing him up on my own and it's been very difficult. He's fifteen and he isn't interested in schoolwork. We argue* all the time because he never does what I ask. I don't know what to do, I really don't.'

'I'm sorry to hear that,' you say. 'Jack's at a difficult age.'

This explains why Sylvia is often worried at work.

'I'm sorry to put you in this situation with the foam letters,' she says. 'It was a mistake* to agree to do it.'

52

'It's OK,' you say. 'I'll sort it out.' You pick up the phone. It is time to speak to Hans.

▶ section 86

Section 89

'That's not what your boss says,' Hans replies. 'Karen sent me an email this morning asking me to arrange it with Sylvia. Karen and I talked about the letters when we had lunch together.'

'I see,' you say. 'OK then, leave it with me. We'll try and fix* it for your daughter's birthday.'

'Thank you so much,' says Hans. 'I knew I could count on you.'

The call ends. Now you need to find someone to make the letters.

Do you ...

1 speak to Eva, the creative director?   ▶ section 92

2 speak to Layla, your copywriter?   ▶ section 93

Section 90

You phone Hans. He sounds delighted*. 'What a party!' he says. 'You really helped me out.'

'How were the letters?' you ask.

'Wonderful!' he says. 'My daughter loved them. I know it wasn't really your job, but you did me a massive* favour*. Thank you. I won't forget this.'

'You're very welcome. You can tell me more about it at the meeting next week.'

'Ah, yes,' Hans asks. 'How's the preparation going?'

'Very well. The creative team have been working on their ideas for the slogan "It's a tough nut to crack." They have some fantastic suggestions.'

'That's good news,' says Hans. 'I'm very excited to hear all your ideas. Well, bye for now. Thank you once again.'

'You're very welcome.' You put the phone down and smile. You have done a great job, but there is no time to relax. It is time to get ready for the next important meeting with the creative team and Hans.

Chapter 5

Section 91

'Karen speaking,' your manager says as she answers the phone.

'Karen,' you say. 'We've got a problem.'

'Oh, no!' she says. 'What's wrong?'

You explain about Hans and the letters. 'That's not a problem!' Karen replies. 'I told Hans we could arrange it. Just speak to the creative director or someone and ask them to do it, OK? I know it's an annoying* little job, but Hans is an important client. We have to do everything we can to keep him happy, OK? Sorry, I have to go now. I'm about to go to another meeting. Speak later.'

Do you ...

1. call Eva, the creative director? ▶ section 92
2. call Layla, your copywriter? ▶ section 93

Section 92

You phone Eva. 'How are things?' she asks.

'Good, thanks,' you say. 'We've got a problem. Can I ask you something?' Quickly, you explain the situation with the foam letters.

'Why's that a problem for me?' Eva asks.

'Well, you're the creative director and I thought you'd know where to buy the letters.'

'We didn't buy the letters, we made them. You get some special foam from the art shop and you cut the letters out. Then you have to make cotton covers for them! It's a big job. It'll take you a day or two to do it.'

'Can your department do it?'

'No, sorry, everyone's too busy. Anyway, it's your job. Good luck!'

She hangs up*.

Do you ...

1. ask Sylvia and all the office staff to stay at work late to make the letters? ▶ section 101
2. pay an art company to make the letters using a company credit card? ▶ section 100

Chapter 5

Section 93

Layla's office is across the corridor so you walk over to see her. She is looking at Facebook and quickly minimises her screen when you go in. She looks nervous and slightly angry to see you. You notice that her hair is red now.

'Hi!' she says. 'What's up?'

Section 94

You feel very happy that you managed to solve the problem. The day after the party you decide to call Hans to see if he was happy with the letters.

Look at the Contacts section on page 186.

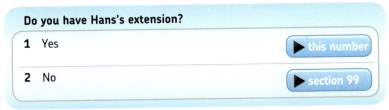

Section 95

After she has listened to you, Layla does not look very concerned*.

'I'm a copywriter*, not a designer,' she says. 'You need to speak to Eva. She's the creative director. Sorry.'

She turns back to her computer and puts on a pair of headphones. As you are leaving the office, you see her screen. Layla is looking at Facebook again.

Section 96

'You're right. Let's think for a minute,' says Layla. You tell her the story about the party and the foam letters with the company names. 'I know!' says Layla.

55

Chapter 5

'We can do this really easily! Last year, we didn't throw those letters away. We packed them in the basement* of this building. I did it with John Miller. There are lots of letters down there. How do you spell her name?' You tell her. 'I'm sure we've got all those letters. Come on. Let's have a look!'

Together, you go down into the basement underneath the offices. The lights are not very bright so it is hard to see. You walk slowly after Layla. 'Aaaargh!' she screams. 'What's that?'

97 Section 97

'Wow, new look!' you say.

'Yeah, I looked in the mirror and I thought, "Why not?". My brother's a hairdresser and he needed to practise for work. So this week, it's red. How can I help you?'

You explain the problem with the letters for Hans's daughter.

'Hmm ... it's not really my job, you know.'

What do you say?

1 'This is for the company! Hans is a really important customer. It's everybody's job.'

2 'I know, but I need all the help I can get.'

98 Section 98

You win 1 bonus point. Mark the scorecard on page 186.

'Yes, of course!' says Hans.

'First of all, what colour would you like?'

'Any colour, actually a mix of colours would be nice,' says Hans.

'And most importantly, your daughter's name. It's Catherine, right?'

'Yes, but it's Katherine with a "K" not a "C". Lots of people misspell* it – I hate it when that happens!'

'OK, got it. I'll let you know when we've got the letters.'

'Great. Look, if you need to contact me again, call me on this extension, 090.'

Write down Hans's extension in the Contacts section on page 186.

56

Chapter 5

Section 99

You phone Avoca and ask to speak to Hans. 'It's you!' he sounds very angry. 'What were you thinking?'

'I'm sorry?' you ask.

'I had two hundred guests at a five-star hotel for my daughter's eighteenth birthday party. When the staff* brought out the letters spelling her name, imagine the reaction when they read "Catherine".'

You suddenly feel very cold. 'Catherine is her name, isn't it?'

'Her name's Katherine with a "K"! You spelt* it wrong!'

'Oh, no! I'm so sorry. Was she upset*?'

'Katherine was OK, but I was humiliated in front of all my friends and family.'

'I ... I don't know what to say. I'm sorry. It won't happen again.'

'You're right. It won't happen again!'

'What are you saying?' you ask.

'I can't trust you. Don't waste* your time working on the Avoca account. We're going to another agency. I shall inform Karen by email.' The call ends.

Your mistake* has lost the Avoca contract!

Go back to the start of the chapter and try again.

 section 83

Section 100

You don't believe Eva, so you look online and you quickly find an art agency. You call them and they agree to make the foam letters for the party. The letters are expensive, but they will look great. The art agency is very professional and they deliver the letters on time. The quality of their work is excellent.

 section 94

Section 101

You call Sylvia and two other junior employees. Feeling nervous, you explain that together they are going to make these letters for Hans's party. The younger employees do not look happy and Sylvia tells you that she doesn't have much time. However, you insist.

Sylvia goes to an art shop to buy the foam and then she buys some coloured cotton sheets. You all work late that night. Sylvia can sew, so she

Chapter 5

uses a sewing machine to make the cotton covers for the letters.

At last, the name is ready. You say 'thank you' to your team and take a taxi home. As you get into bed, you look at your alarm clock. The time is 3.00 a.m.

102 Section 102

There is something covering Layla's head. You touch it. 'It's OK!' you say. 'It's only a spider's web.'

'Argh! I hate spiders!'

You pull the sticky spider's web off Layla and rub it off your hands. 'We need a torch*,' you say.

'I'll go!' Layla says quickly, and she runs back up the stairs.

You wait in the basement for a few minutes. Your eyes get accustomed to the dark and you start to look around for the letters. Suddenly, a hand slaps your shoulder. You scream, and close your eyes. Then you hear laughter. 'Ha, ha! Scared you! It's only me,' says Layla. She shines the torch and, hidden at the back of the room, you see a big pile of letters.

'Over there!' you shout. The letters are huge* and very dusty. Eventually, you find a brush and you clean them. Dusted, the letters look like new and they are a mix of different colours. 'Layla, you've done it!' you say. 'This is fantastic.'

'You owe me,' she replies.

You find the right letters and you send them by courier to the hotel for Hans's party.

▶ section 94

Chapter 6

Section 103

You have butterflies* in your stomach again, but this time it is because you are excited. Today, you and the creative team are pitching* three possible TV adverts to Hans Fischer. You have spent two weeks working on different ideas for the 'tough nut* to crack' ad for the Avoca Arrow. You are really confident* about the final selection, and you feel sure Hans will like them too. Hans is supposed to meet you in reception at the Clifton Creative Agency office at 9.30, but he is late. Suddenly you realise you have a voicemail message on your mobile phone.

'Hello, hello. Yes this is Hans here. *Verdammt*! In this city the streets are like an *Autobahn* – a highway*! Back home in Cologne, in Germany, the city is much more pedestrian-friendly ... I will be at your office in five minutes if I can just cross this street. OK? See you in a minute.'

Eventually, Hans arrives and comes into reception. His face is red and he wipes a handkerchief across his forehead. 'So much traffic!' he says.

'Yes, the traffic's really busy here in the mornings,' you say. 'Isn't Dagmar coming today?'

'No, she has dog flu,' says Hans.

'I'm sorry,' you say.

'So are we meeting in the boardroom* today?' asks Hans.

'Actually, we're going out. We're going to catch a ferry into Sydney city centre.'

'Oh no!' says Hans. 'Do we have to cross that street again?'

Section 104

You ask the receptionist to call the team and then you all drive in two Avoca cars down to the Manly ferry. From the Clifton offices, there are you, John Miller, Sylvia Watson and the creative team – Eva Campano, and the copywriter Layla Evans.

You are alone in the car with Hans. He starts to ask you about your work. 'I hear your company has a contract with Gondwanaland,' he says. 'How's business there?'

Chapter 6

This is true. Gondwanaland is a popular tourist destination in the north of Australia and Clifton handles the account with the Tourism Board. You know quite a lot about this account because your friend Pete Deng works there.

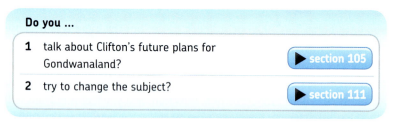

105 Section 105

You talk a lot about the Gondwanaland account. You tell Hans about its successes and failures and what the plans are for the future. Hans listens and nods*. Finally, he coughs. 'I'm very happy that the account with Gondwanaland is going well,' he says. 'But I hope you don't talk about Avoca like this. We take company confidentiality very seriously.'

'Er … no, of course not,' you say. 'I just wanted to explain a little about Clifton.' You feel embarrassed*. You have talked too much about Clifton's work with other clients*, and Hans is nervous. The day has not started well. Hans looks at his watch.

'We're nearly there,' you say.

106 Section 106

Eva stands up to present the 'safe' idea. 'So, we start with an image of an Avoca Arrow in Sydney. It's a hot day and the car is driving through heavy traffic. There are trucks, vans, buses and lots of other vehicles on the roads. It looks difficult but the Avoca Arrow negotiates the traffic easily.' Hans folds his arms. He doesn't look impressed*. You feel nervous as Eva continues her description. 'All the time, we see little bits of the driver. In the beginning, it's the back of his head. Then, his hands and his watch. Then, a close up of his eyes. Finally, he gets out of the car and we see it's a famous actor.'

You add, 'Our focus groups tell us that the most popular male actor for a car with an image like the Arrow is Daniel Craig, so we would look for someone like him.'

Chapter 6

Eva continues, 'He's a tough man and he stands outside the car. The slogan* appears: "The Avoca Arrow. It's a tough nut to crack." That's it.'

Hans shakes his head. 'No, no, no,' he says. 'This is a stereotype. All the car adverts are like this. I don't like it at all.'

Do you ....

1 defend the advert? ▶ section 113

2 move on to the next advert? ▶ section 114

Section 107

107

The sea is calm this morning. The air smells fresh and cool. The half-hour ferry journey is very relaxing. Hundreds of people wearing summer clothes are walking around the deck of the boat as it travels past Sydney Opera House. Eventually you arrive at Darling Harbour*.

A hundred years ago, Darling Harbour was a busy port with big warehouses and dozens of ships. These days it is mainly an area for restaurants and entertainment, although it still looks quite industrial. You have booked* a meeting room in a luxurious hotel opposite an old power station. You chose this destination for your presentation carefully. Clients are more enthusiastic about ideas when they are presented in an unusual location that relates to the ad campaign*. You think the urban environment around the hotel will help Hans understand your ideas.

'So,' says Hans, 'here we all are. I'm keen* to know what ideas you have come up with. I hope that after all, this campaign has not been "a tough nut to crack"!' He laughs, but you are shaking when you stand up to give your presentation. This is a critical moment for the company.

Section 108

108

You look around the room. Seated at the table are your colleagues. John Miller is chewing* gum* and looking serious. Sylvia is ready to take notes. Eva and Layla are looking nervous.

When the creative team produce an advert, they always develop three ideas. One is the 'safe' idea, which is easy-to-understand, but not very original. Next is the 'fun' idea, which is new, unusual and entertaining.

61

Chapter 6

And finally the 'risky' idea, which is very creative, but a little crazy too – it is the kind of ad that might win an industry award, but most clients probably won't accept.

You must decide on the best order so your favourite idea looks good and Hans will accept it.

109 Section 109

The 'risky' idea is a dramatic advert. It contains lots of crazy action and some violence.

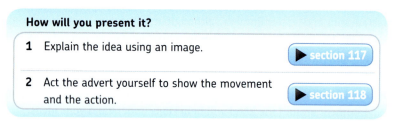

110 Section 110

The 'fun' idea is actually your favourite idea. Hans sips his coffee while he listens to you. 'Right,' you say. 'This is a fun idea that we think will really work. Eva?'

'This time,' says Eva. 'We have a guy aged about 18. At the beginning of the advert, he asks to borrow his uncle's car for the evening. His uncle is about 30 years old and very cool*. The uncle says, "OK, but don't go crazy!" and the young guy says, "Of course not," with a big smile. Afterwards, we see the car in the outback, you know, the Australian countryside.'

'So, the advert will be in the Australian desert?' asks Hans. He looks very interested.

Chapter 6

'That's right,' says Eva. 'So the nephew goes completely crazy driving really hard in the outback, rolling the car, driving through a river and so on. It ends up with a play fight with a crocodile.'

Hans smiles. 'A crocodile – interesting,' he says.

'Finally, we see the guy driving back to his uncle's house,' says Eva. 'The uncle asks, "Was the car OK?" and the nephew says, "Yeah, no problems." He looks as if he has been on a 20-km run – he's sweating* and

his clothes are all dirty. He laughs nervously while his uncle is inspecting the car. But the car is perfect, it's completely clean, it looks like new. We end with a shot of the Avoca Arrow outside the house with the slogan*, "The Avoca Arrow – a tough nut to crack." What do you think?'

'Well, OK, that's a nice idea,' says Hans. 'Show me what else you have.'

section 131

Section 111

111

'Gondwanaland is a great destination for tourists,' you say. 'Actually, today we're going to another interesting tourist spot – one here in Sydney. We thought it would be the perfect place to present our ideas for the Avoca campaign to you.'

Hans smiles and nods his head. 'So you're changing the subject because you can't talk about other company accounts, right?'

'Something like that,' you say.

'I appreciate* that,' says Hans. 'It's very professional. I don't want Clifton people telling everyone about Avoca.'

'I completely agree,' you reply. 'We respect client* confidentiality, so we don't talk about our current* projects to anyone outside the company.'

'It's essential*' says Hans. 'I respect you. You come from the auto industry*, so you really know how our business works – not like these advertising people.'

'Well, I think the team will have some good ideas for you today, Hans.'

You arrive at the Manly ferry terminal.

section 107

63

Chapter 6

112 Section 112

⭐ You win 1 bonus point. Mark the scorecard on page 186.

'Yes, I think it's a brilliant ad,' says Hans. 'Just brilliant! I think it's exciting, young, fun and it communicates our message successfully. You've done it!' He starts clapping*. 'I congratulate you and your team,' he says. Everyone smiles and they start clapping too.

You presented the adverts in exactly the right order. You thought the fun ad was the best idea so you presented it last. The safe choice was never going to be Hans's favourite. However, it was a sensible way to start the meeting before you showed the more original ideas. You knew the risky advert was a bit crazy, but it made the fun idea look good.

Excellent decision!

113 Section 113

'There are lots of adverts like this because they work,' you say. 'Our focus groups and our research* show–'

'Your focus groups!' says Hans. 'I'm not interested in your focus groups. If you ask the public for ideas, they just describe the ads that they have seen in the past. I want to do something new. I want to surprise people.'

'What you want to do is sell cars,' you say, 'and this advert will work.'

'Look, you worked in the auto industry*,' says Hans, 'and you know that the choice of advertising campaign is not my decision alone. I have to go to the Board of Avoca and get their approval for the campaign too. I can't present an advert that I don't believe in myself. I'm sorry, but I can't present this advert to my company. Do you know how competitive the car industry is these days? We have to fight just to keep the same market share.'

'I understand,' you say. 'Don't worry, we have some more creative ideas for you.'

'Good,' says Hans. 'I knew I could depend on you.'

'OK, let's move on to the next idea,' you say.

64

Chapter 6

Section 114

Which advert idea will you present next?

1. The risky idea — ▶ section 115
2. The fun idea — ▶ section 110

Section 115

The 'risky' idea is a dramatic advert. It contains lots of crazy action and some violence.

How will you present it?

1. Explain the idea using an image. — ▶ section 121
2. Act the advert yourself to show the movement and the action. — ▶ section 118

Section 116

You have presented all three advert ideas to Hans. He has rejected* the 'safe' idea, but he likes the 'risky' action movie idea and the 'fun' crocodile idea.

'So where are we?' asks Hans. 'Which of these two adverts do you think will work for the Avoca Arrow?'

Do you ...

1. suggest the risky idea? — ▶ section 120
2. suggest the fun idea? — ▶ section 124

65

Chapter 6

117 Section 117

Eva puts an image in front of Hans and explains the advert. 'Imagine the scene,' she says. 'It's night in the city. Suddenly the Avoca Arrow appears.

It moves incredibly fast through the street. Then, we see the street is full of criminals. They start shooting at the car. The car races through a fire too, but nothing can damage* it. Finally, it escapes the street, but another car follows it – it's a race! First the Avoca Arrow is in front and then the other car, but the other car's going too fast, so it rolls over onto its side. The driver gets out just before the car explodes. Only the Avoca Arrow survives. It's like an action movie. What do you think?'

'Yes, interesting,' Hans says. He puts his hands together and presses the tops of his fingers against his lips. He is clearly thinking very hard.

Which idea will you show Hans next?

1 The fun idea — ▶ section 122

2 The safe idea — ▶ section 125

118 Section 118

The 'risky' idea is like an action movie or a computer game. The Avoca Arrow is driving through a very dangerous part of the city. People try to attack the car. To escape, the driver has to twist and turn to the right and left and drive very quickly.

To make the presentation more exciting, you decide to act out the exciting parts. You jump up as if you are in the car and you accidentally* hit a shelf behind you. There is a glass sculpture of a peacock on the shelf. It falls down to the table, just where Hans is sitting.

▶ section 119

Chapter 6

Section 119

119

'Look out!' you shout.

'What?' asks Hans. He doesn't understand you and he hasn't seen the peacock. With a loud crash, it shatters into a thousand tiny pieces on the table. There is glass everywhere. Hans touches a piece and cuts his hand badly. 'Ow!' he shouts.

'Are you OK?' you ask.

'Of course I'm not OK!' Hans shouts. 'Look at my hand!' There is a lot of blood and it is dripping onto the table.

'Come with me,' says Sylvia. 'We need the first aid box and then you should go to hospital. That's a very nasty cut.'

'Yes, Sylvia, thank you,' says Hans and he follows her out of the room.

You look at the rest of the team. They are OK but there is broken glass and blood all over your papers.

'It looks like this meeting is over,' says John.

'Next time, let me give the client presentation, OK?' says Eva.

'I'm so sorry, everyone,' you say. No one responds. Ten minutes later, a taxi arrives and you watch Hans getting into it with a large bandage around his hand. The meeting has ended in disaster.

Later, when you try to phone and email Hans to apologise* and to arrange another meeting, he doesn't reply.

You have lost one of Clifton's most important clients! You also have a very expensive bill* for the broken sculpture.

Go back to the start of the chapter and try again.

67

Chapter 6

120 Section 120

Hans raises his eyebrows in surprise. 'I'm a bit worried about it,' he says. 'But I think you're right. We'll go with this "risky" ad then. It seems this meeting is over. Thank you very much for all your hard work.' After Hans leaves, everyone goes to lunch. There is a great atmosphere among the team.

'Well I think that's a winner,' says John.

'The meeting went very well,' agrees Sylvia.

'Personally, I'm delighted*,' says Eva. 'Do you know how many times our creative ideas get rejected* by the client? Now we have a really new one. We could win an award from this ad because it's so different.'

'Do you really think so?' asks Layla.

'I do,' says Eva. 'I've never known a client to accept such a radical idea.'

'Me neither,' agrees John. 'Come on, everyone, we've got something to celebrate today!'

Everyone is happy, but you start to worry. Perhaps this advert is too risky? Two weeks pass and you receive no information from Hans. Finally, at 5.00 on a Friday afternoon, you get an email from Avoca Autos.

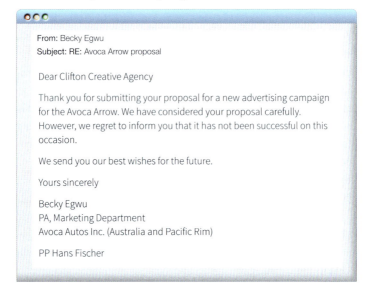

Your proposal has failed and you have lost one of Clifton's biggest customers!

Go back to the start of the chapter and try again.

Chapter 6

Section 121

Eva puts an image in front of Hans and explains the advert. 'Imagine the scene,' she says. 'It's night in the city. Suddenly the Avoca Arrow appears. It moves incredibly fast through the street. Then, we see the street is full of criminals. They start shooting at the car. The car races through a fire too, but nothing can damage* it. Finally, it escapes the street, but another car follows it – it's a race! First the Avoca Arrow is in front and then the other car,

but the other car's going too fast, so it rolls over onto its side. The driver gets out just before the car explodes. Only the Avoca Arrow survives. It's like an action movie. What do you think?'

Hans's face is white. His fingers are tapping* the table. 'This is absurd*,' he says, 'and what's more, it's illegal. We aren't allowed to show races, speeding* and all this violence in a car advert. The government won't permit this.'

'That's right,' agrees John Miller. 'I told them that, but no one listens to me.'

'If people listened to you more,' says Hans, 'the meetings would be quicker. We wouldn't waste time on unrealistic ideas.'

'I agree,' says John and he looks at you.

'Er, perhaps we should look at the last idea? The fun idea?' you suggest.

▶ section 123

Section 122

The 'fun' idea is actually your favourite idea. Hans sips his coffee while he listens to you. 'Right,' you say. 'This is a fun idea that we think will really work. Eva?'

'This time,' says Eva. 'We have a guy aged about 18. At the beginning of the advert, he asks to borrow his uncle's car for the evening. His uncle is about 30 years old and very cool*. The uncle says, "OK, but don't go crazy!" and the young guy says, "Of course not," with a big smile. Afterwards, we see the car

Chapter 6

in the outback, you know, the Australian countryside.'

'So, the advert will be in the Australian desert?' asks Hans. He looks very interested.

'That's right,' says Eva. 'So the nephew goes completely crazy driving really hard in the outback, rolling the car, driving through a river and so on. It ends up with a play fight with a crocodile.'

Hans smiles. 'A crocodile – interesting,' he says.

'Finally, we see the guy driving back to his uncle's house,' says Eva. 'The uncle asks, "Was the car OK?" and the nephew says, "Yeah, no problems." He looks as if he has been on a 20km run – he's sweating* and his clothes are all dirty. He laughs nervously while his uncle is inspecting the car. But the car is perfect, it's completely clean, it looks like new. We end with a shot of the Avoca Arrow outside the house with the slogan*, "The Avoca Arrow – a tough nut to crack." What do you think?'

'Well, OK, that's a nice idea,' says Hans. 'There was one more idea, wasn't there.'

It is time to present the 'safe' idea.

123 Section 123

'This is our final campaign idea,' you say. 'Eva?'

'Thanks,' says Eva. 'Well, here is our third suggestion. This time we have a guy aged about 18. At the beginning of the advert, he asks to borrow his uncle's car for the evening. His uncle is about 30 years old and very cool*. The uncle says, "OK, but don't go crazy!" and the young guy says, "Of course not," with a big smile. Afterwards, we see the car in the outback, you know, the Australian countryside.'

'So, the advert will be in the Australian desert?' asks Hans. He looks very interested.

'That's right,' says Eva. 'So the nephew goes completely crazy driving really hard in the outback, rolling the car, driving through a river and so on. It ends up with a play fight with a crocodile.'

70

Chapter 6

Hans smiles. 'A crocodile – interesting,' he says.

'Finally, we see the guy driving back to his uncle's house,' says Eva. 'The uncle asks, "Was the car OK?" and the nephew says, "Yeah, no problems." He looks as if he has been on a 20-km run – he's sweating* and his clothes are all dirty. He laughs nervously while his uncle is inspecting the car. But the car is perfect, it's completely clean, it looks like new. We end with a shot of the Avoca Arrow outside the house with the slogan*, "The Avoca Arrow – a tough nut to crack." What do you think?'

The meeting room goes silent. Everyone looks at Hans.

Section 124

'Yes, I think it's a good ad,' says Hans. 'Very good!'

'So are you giving us the green light to go ahead with this advert?' you ask.

'I'll check it with my Board,' says Hans, 'but I'm confident* we have our advert and we're ready to go.'

'Great news, Hans,' you say. 'Excellent work, everybody.'

'I have just have one more question,' asks Hans. Nobody speaks. Hans leaves a pause. 'What time's lunch?' he asks. Everyone laughs. The meeting has been a success!

Section 125

Eva stands up to present the 'safe' idea. 'So, we start with an image of an Avoca Arrow in Sydney. It's a hot day and the car is driving through heavy traffic. There are trucks, vans, buses and lots of other vehicles on the roads. It looks difficult but the Avoca Arrow negotiates the traffic easily.' Hans folds his arms. He doesn't look impressed*. You feel nervous as Eva continues her description. 'All the time, we see little bits of the driver. In the beginning, it's the back of his head. Then his hands and his watch. Then a close up of his eyes. Finally, he gets out of the car and we see it's a famous actor …'

Hans shakes his head. 'No, no, no,' he says. 'This is a stereotype*. All car adverts are like this. I don't like it at all. This one will not be our advert. I'm sorry. Don't you have any better ideas?'

71

Chapter 6

Section 126

'Right,' you say. 'This is a fun idea that we think will really work. Eva?'

'This time,' says Eva. 'We have a guy aged about 18. At the beginning of the advert, he asks to borrow his uncle's car for the evening. His uncle is about 30 years old and very cool*. The uncle says, "OK, but don't go crazy!" and the young guy says, "Of course not," with a big smile. Afterwards, we see the car in the outback, you know, the Australian countryside.'

'So, the advert will be in the Australian desert?' asks Hans. He looks very interested.

'That's right,' says Eva. 'So the nephew goes completely crazy driving really hard in the outback, rolling the car, driving through a river and so on. It ends up with a play fight with a crocodile.'

Hans smiles. 'A crocodile – interesting,' he says.

'Finally, we see the guy driving back to his uncle's house,' says Eva. 'The uncle asks, "Was the car OK?" and the nephew says, "Yeah, no problems." He looks as if he has been on a 20-km run – he's sweating* and his clothes are all dirty. He laughs nervously while his uncle is inspecting the car. But the car is perfect, it's completely clean, it looks like new. We end with a shot of the Avoca Arrow outside the house with the slogan*, "The Avoca Arrow – a tough nut to crack." What do you think?'

'Ha!' says Hans. 'I like it. It's very adventurous. But come on, I think you have some other ideas, don't you? Show me your craziest idea for the ad.'

You have to show Hans the 'risky' idea now.

Section 127

Eva stands up. 'I think you will like this idea. We have a young guy, about eighteen years old. He asks to borrow his uncle's car for the evening. His uncle is about 30 years old and very cool*. The uncle says, "OK, but don't go crazy!" and the young guy says, "Of course not," with a big smile.

Chapter 6

Afterwards, we see the car in the outback, you know, the Australian countryside.'

'So, the advert will be in the Australian desert?' asks Hans. He looks very interested.

'That's right,' says Eva. 'So the nephew goes completely crazy driving really hard in the outback, rolling the car, driving through a river and so on. It ends up with a play fight with a crocodile.'

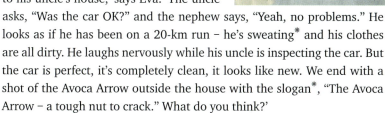

Hans smiles. 'A crocodile – interesting,' he says.

'Finally, we see the guy driving back to his uncle's house,' says Eva. 'The uncle asks, "Was the car OK?" and the nephew says, "Yeah, no problems." He looks as if he has been on a 20-km run – he's sweating* and his clothes are all dirty. He laughs nervously while his uncle is inspecting the car. But the car is perfect, it's completely clean, it looks like new. We end with a shot of the Avoca Arrow outside the house with the slogan*, "The Avoca Arrow – a tough nut to crack." What do you think?'

'I like it,' says Hans, 'but I liked the first idea too.'

Section 128

128

Your 'risky' idea is a dramatic advert. The ad idea contains lots of crazy action and some violence.

How will you present it?

1 Explain the idea using an image.

2 Act the advert yourself to show the movement and the action.

Section 129

129

Eva puts an image in front of Hans and explains the advert. 'Imagine the scene,' she says. 'It's night in the city. Suddenly the Avoca Arrow appears.

Chapter 6

It moves incredibly fast through the street. Then, we see the street is full of criminals. They start shooting at the car. The car races through a fire too, but nothing can damage it. Finally, it escapes the street, but another

car follows it – it's a race! First the Avoca Arrow is in front and then the other car, but the other car's going too fast, so it rolls over onto its side. The driver gets out just before the car explodes. Only the Avoca Arrow survives. It's like an action movie. What do you think?'

'Well that's different,' says Hans. 'But I prefer the first ad. The one with the young man and the crocodile. Let's go with that shall we?'

'Actually,' says John, 'we have one more idea. It's a safer idea.'

'No, I'm not interested in safe ideas,' says Hans.

'I think you should see it,' says John.

Hans looks at you.

Do you …

1 insist on showing Hans the safe idea?

2 say that you prefer the fun idea with the crocodile too?

130 Section 130

Eva stands up and presents the 'safe' idea. Hans is clearly not interested and he starts tidying up his folders. When Eva finishes, he looks around the table.

'The same old ideas again,' he says. 'I've been in this business for many years and I always see the same ad ideas. I wonder what we are paying you for.'

'It's not the best idea,' you agree, 'but it is a good one. Let's go to lunch and discuss it.'

'I'm sorry,' says Hans, 'I don't have a lot of time for lunch today.'

Chapter 6

The meeting ends. You are optimistic* because Hans liked one of your ads, but he changed his mind* a lot at the end of the meeting.

The next day, you are shocked* to receive an email from his company.

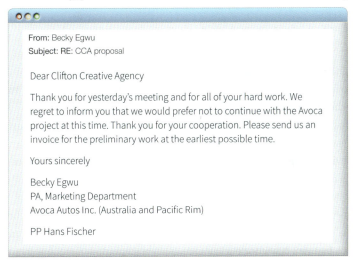

From: Becky Egwu
Subject: RE: CCA proposal

Dear Clifton Creative Agency

Thank you for yesterday's meeting and for all of your hard work. We regret to inform you that we would prefer not to continue with the Avoca project at this time. Thank you for your cooperation. Please send us an invoice for the preliminary work at the earliest possible time.

Yours sincerely

Becky Egwu
PA, Marketing Department
Avoca Autos Inc. (Australia and Pacific Rim)

PP Hans Fischer

You have lost one of Clifton's most important clients!

Go back to the start of the chapter and try again.

Section 131

Eva stands up to present the final, 'risky' idea. She looks enthusiastic and she presents this idea with a lot more energy. It is an advert where the Avoca auto drives through a violent city in the future. After just two minutes, Hans puts his hand up. 'Stop! Stop, please,' he says. 'We can't do this advert because it's too violent. The board of Avoca don't approve of adverts like this. No, I'm sorry.' Eva looks furious*. She stares* at you but Hans is still talking. 'No, I don't like this advert at all,' he says, 'but I do like the advert with the young guy and the crocodile. I think it's just fantastic, and I will present that to my board.'

'Really?' asks John.

'That's fantastic news!' you say.

'Yes, I love it,' says Hans. 'It's much better than all this violence and fighting. In fact, I'm sure that they'll accept it. Well done everybody! I

Chapter 6

think we have our advert for the Avoca Arrow!'

Everyone claps* and they begin to leave the meeting room. Eva waits until everyone has gone and then talks to you.

132 Section 132

'You did it all wrong!' says Eva.

'What do you mean?' you ask. 'Hans accepted one of our ideas. We've won the contract!'

'Yes,' says Eva, 'but the risky idea was more exciting. It was a mistake to present it at the end. He wasn't listening properly.'

'It doesn't matter,' you say. 'Hans loves the fun idea. We've saved the Avoca contract.'

'Good for you,' says Eva. 'But I'm not happy.'

Fortunately, Hans comes back into the room. 'Come on everybody! Lunch time!' he says. 'Let's celebrate our success. It was "a tough nut to crack", but you have done it!'

The meeting has been a success and you have saved the Avoca contract, even if Eva is not happy about it.

Chapter 7

Section 133

It is a warm evening. Apart from the moon, the only other light is coming from your neighbour's house. You can hear their TV. The volume seems to get louder every time the adverts come on. You turn on your laptop* and see you have a message from your friend Pete Deng.

'Hi! How are things? I'm really busy ... again! We're getting lots of requests for information from the press. I have to speak to about six journalists a day and my boss, Anastasia, is never here! She spends most her time on research* trips – usually in five-star hotels! So even though I live in paradise, I spend all of my time in the office! Anyway, give me a call if you go online later. I'm working late at the office tonight, so I'll be connected. Speak to you later!'

You see Pete is connected and you call him. 'Hi Pete, are you still at work?'

'Yes. Crazy isn't it! I've almost finished though. How are things?'

'Work's going well. I've got a meeting to present our final plans for a TV advert tomorrow morning.'

'Sounds interesting.'

'Yes, we're going to show the client* all the different scenes for the ad. If he approves* them, then we're going to film it in the Australian outback.'

'Great. I suppose you have a cool* soundtrack for the ad.'

'Soundtrack?'

'Yes, the music that goes with the action.'

'I hadn't thought about music. Thanks Pete, that's a great idea.'

Chapter 7

134 Section 134

You log on to YouTube to find the video that Layla was playing. Layla says it is what all the young people are listening to these days, and you can imagine the Avoca Arrow driving fast with this music in the background*. The meeting starts soon, so you collect your papers and your laptop* and go to the boardroom*.

▶ section 147

135 Section 135

'Mr Fischer,' says Eva. 'I'd like to show you some drawings of the TV ad. This is the storyboard we're going to film in a few weeks. If there are any small things you'd like to change, now is the time to ask. We can't change the plans once we're filming on location*.'

'Of course,' he agrees. 'That's standard industry practice.'

Eva begins her presentation. 'First, we see an image of the Avoca Arrow outside a normal house. The car looks very new and shiny. Then we see the nephew and the uncle. The nephew smiles and asks, "Can I borrow your car?" and the uncle says, "Yes, sure. But be careful!" Then we see the nephew walking towards the car. He looks into the driver's window and we see the smile on his face. He presses the key fob and he jumps a little when the lights flash and the alarm makes a loud noise.'

▶ section 136

Section 136

'Next we see the nephew sitting in the driver's seat of the car. He looks around and then presses the Start button. Then we have an outside shot of the car from the front, we can see the nephew through the windscreen. He has a big smile on his face. We can hear the loud sound of the engine – vroom, vroom!' says Eva, making car engine noises. Hans laughs, and then Karen and everyone else laugh. 'Next, we're back inside the car. The nephew laughs quietly and says, "Yes!" Then the camera moves further away. We see the nephew driving the Avoca Arrow carefully into the street. After that, we see the back of the car as it drives away from the uncle's house.'

▶ section 153

Section 137

⭐ You win 1 bonus point. Mark the scorecard on page 186.
You open YouTube and play the song that Karen chose.

Hans nods* his head and starts to act playing the guitar with his hands.

'I love it!' says Hans smiling. 'This music is perfect for the Arrow ad, you obviously understand our target* audience very well. I'm impressed*.'

▶ section 138

Chapter 7

138 Section 138

Eva continues describing the advert, 'While he's driving, he suddenly sees some sheep in the road. He turns very quickly to avoid* hitting the animals, and the car goes onto two wheels!'

'Will people complain about that?' asks Hans.

'Ah!' says Eva. 'We can do this using computer images, so no animals will get hurt. At the end of this very exciting and fast-moving action sequence, we see the nephew at the wheel of the car. He has wide eyes and a huge* smile on his face.'

▶ section 139

139 Section 139

'We end back in the city, with the nephew driving the Avoca Arrow back to the uncle's house. He looks exhausted* and he's covered in dust. Next, we see him giving back the key to his uncle, who looks really worried and says, "You look terrible! What happened?" The nephew says, "Not much. Just a quick ride". The uncle says goodbye, and we have a close-up of his face. Then he begins to smile. We end with the same scene as the beginning – the car looking perfect and brand-new. The voice-over says, "The Avoca Arrow – a tough nut to crack!".'

Hans starts to clap* slowly. You aren't sure how to react. Neither is John. Then you notice that Hans has a big smile on his face. He stands up and starts to clap more quickly. 'Bravo!' he shouts. 'I love it!'

'Great!' you say. 'We're very pleased with it too.'

'But where is my crocodile? I thought the boy was going to have a fight with a crocodile?'

'Ah, yes, the crocodile. We realised it would be too hard to film, but don't worry, the ad works really well without the crocodile.'

'But I want the crocodile!'

What do you say?

1 'Of course! The customer's always right. We'll include a crocodile fight.' ▶ section 140

2 'I honestly think the ad will be better without it.' ▶ section 141

Section 140

140

'Good,' says Hans. 'I loved that crocodile idea! The ad will be perfect with that bit.'

Your colleagues look at you angrily, but they don't say anything. After the meeting, Hans leaves with Dagmar. Eva and John look at you and shout, 'WHAT?' at the same time.

'That was a really silly thing to say. Where are we going to find a crocodile?' asks Eva. 'It'll be really expensive to use computer generated images.'

'I don't know,' you say. 'I thought you might know somebody.'

'You agreed to a crocodile.' Eva stands up angrily. 'Either you find one or you tell Hans that we can't do that scene.'

'But I've just told him we could do it.'

Chapter 7

'That's not my problem.' Eva and John walk out of the meeting room.

Sylvia starts to collect the coffee cups. 'You made a mistake* there,' she says.

'I know,' you reply.

'Look, maybe I can help you. We've worked with a company that makes life-size model animals before. They're incredibly realistic. I'm sure they've got a model crocodile you could hire for the ad.'

'Really?' you say enthusiastically.

'The company's called Technix.' I have a contact number somewhere.' Sylvia looks on her phone and writes down a number on a piece of paper. 'Call Geoff, his extension's 190, see if he can help.'

 Go to the Contacts section on page 186 and write down Geoff's extension at Technix.

When you get back to your desk you phone Technix and speak to Geoff. They have two different model crocodiles you can use – one for close-ups and one for the fight scene. 'Thanks Geoff,' you say at the end of the conversation, 'you've just saved my job.'

Later, you send an email to the team telling them that you have solved the crocodile problem.

141 Section 141

'Why?' asks Hans. 'The crocodile was my favourite bit!'

'It didn't work,' you explain. 'If the driver fights a crocodile, he has to get out of the car. How? We thought about the car door opening accidentally*, and the driver falling out of the car. But then people will think the doors of the Arrow don't work properly*.' Hans thinks for a second. 'Trust us, Hans. The ad doesn't need the crocodile.'

'OK, I understand,' says Hans. 'I agree. No crocodile.'

After the meeting, Hans leaves with Dagmar.

'Well done! I was worried about what Hans would say,' says Eva.

'And where would we get a crocodile from?' says Karen. 'Phew! You've saved the day.'

82

Chapter 7

Section 142

142

You arrive at work early the next day to prepare for the meeting. You are surprised to see John sitting at his desk. 'Hi John,' you say. 'We need some music to use in the Avoca presentation. You've seen the storyboards for the ad. Have you got any music that we could use?'

'Good idea!' he says, opening a drawer and taking out some CDs. He gives one to you. 'Try this,' he says. 'Track number 3.' You take the CD. It is a classical music compilation. You put the CD into your computer and play track 3.

'It's the perfect music to go with the ad,' he says. 'It's powerful and emotional.'

'Thanks, John,' you say. You decide to ask a few other people what they think.

Section 143

143

You call Layla. 'Hi, we need some music for the Avoca presentation. Have you got anything suitable?'

'Sure. Come round.' You go to Layla's office and she is online. She turns up the volume on her computer and starts dancing.

'What's this?'

She looks at her computer and then at you, 'I don't know, but it's good though!'

'Great. Can you email me the details?' you say.

You are walking back to your office when you bump into* Karen.

Section 144

144

You explain to Karen that you need some music for the Avoca presentation. 'I have exactly the right music for you,' she says. She takes her phone out of her handbag and then holds it up. 'Listen to this.' It is rock music.

'Really?' you ask.

Karen smiles and says, 'Trust me.' You go to get a cup of coffee.

83

Chapter 7

Section 145

You are standing by the coffee machine when Sylvia walks into work. She is wearing a tracksuit and she looks as if she has been jogging*. You tell her about the music choices and ask, 'What do you think, Sylvia?'

She takes off her headphones and gives them to you. You put them over your ears. It is a song by a well-known pop group. 'Why not use something that everyone can enjoy?' she advises.

You now have four music recommendations for the Avoca presentation.

Which music do you choose?

1	John's classical music	▶ section 146
2	Layla's dance music	▶ section 134
3	Karen's rock music	▶ section 148
4	Sylvia's pop music	▶ section 152

Section 146

You find an old CD player in a cupboard and listen to track 3 of John's classical CD again. It is very powerful and you can imagine the Avoca Arrow driving fast with this music in the background*. You smile. The meeting starts soon, so you collect your papers and the CD player and go to the boardroom*.

Section 147

Everyone is in the boardroom* waiting for Hans to arrive. 'Good morning,' you say. 'As Hans isn't here yet, why don't we make a start on item three on the agenda*? Eva, can you give us an update* on the–'

All of a sudden, there is a loud noise in the corridor. The door opens and Hans falls into the meeting room followed by the receptionist holding Dagmar. Hans is breathing heavily and looks very hot in his white suit.

'The traffic here!' he says between breaths. 'It's too much! My poor little Dagmar, she can't run fast enough.' Dagmar suddenly starts barking*. Layla

Chapter 7

and Eva cover their ears. The receptionist takes Dagmar out of the room. Sylvia brings in coffee and biscuits and the meeting starts.

section 135

Section 148

You log on to YouTube to find the song that Karen was playing. You are surprised that Karen has music like this on her phone, but you are sure she made the right choice. It has a really good rhythm and heavy guitars, and you can imagine the Avoca Arrow driving fast with this music in the background*. The meeting starts soon, so you collect your papers and your laptop* and go to the boardroom*.

section 147

Section 149

You plug Sylvia's MP3 player into the speakers and play the song. Hans looks at you, holds up his hand and says, 'stop!'

'We wanted music that everybody would like,' you explain.

'Well, why are we listening to this boring song that nobody will like?' asks Hans. 'Boring, boring, boring! Is that what you think of the Arrow?'

'Of course not, Hans! We also have this,' says Karen, and she puts her phone on the table and plays the rock song.

Hans starts to nod his head to the music. 'This is it!' says Hans. 'It's perfect!'

section 138

Section 150

You press 'play' on the CD player and the classical music that John gave you fills the room. Hans looks at you and then at Karen. He shakes his head. 'Enough!' he shouts. 'This isn't any good for this ad! We need something loud, something that the target audience will find exciting.'

Without speaking, Karen passes you her phone. You look at the screen. It is ready to play the rock song that she recommended.

Hans starts to nod* his head to the music. 'This is better!' he says. 'This music fits the ad!'

section 138

85

Chapter 7

151 Section 151

You open your laptop, find Layla's song online and play it. Loud dance music fills the room. Hans looks at you and then closes his eyes. 'Stop!' he shouts. 'What is this music? Who likes this music? I mean, imagine you're watching TV and then this … this "music" attacks! No! It's too horrible.'

'You're right, Hans. We also have this,' says Karen as she passes you her phone. You look at the screen. It is ready to play the rock song.

Hans starts to nod his head to the music. 'I like this,' he says. 'This music is much better for the Arrow ad.'

152 Section 152

You plug Sylvia's MP3 player into some speakers and listen to the song that she played to you. 'If Sylvia likes this song then everyone should like it,' you think. It is a very nice tune and you can imagine the Avoca Arrow driving fast with this music in the background*. The meeting starts soon, so you collect your papers and the speakers and go to the boardroom*.

153 Section 153

'For the next ten seconds, we have some exciting action with the car being driven fast through the outback,' says Eva.

'We're thinking of using some music like this,' you say.

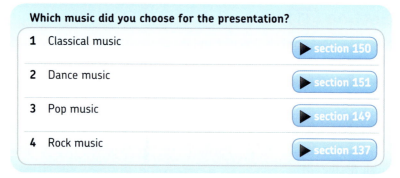

86

Chapter 8

Section 154

It feels great to finally go to work without butterflies* in your stomach. Avoca Autos has approved* the concept for the Arrow TV ad. Now, your job is to make sure that the production process goes smoothly*. A production company is going to film the TV ad. After that, the magazine, poster and digital campaigns can be produced using photos taken from the TV ad.

A location scout* is in central Australia looking for the perfect place to film* the ad, and you are about to take your first business trip out there. You are flying to Alice Springs and you are excited about the trip. Unfortunately, Hans wants to come too. You remember you were hired to keep Avoca Autos as a client and Karen thinks you are the best person to keep Hans happy.

You are walking through reception when suddenly, you see a face you recognise* – it is Ryan Gosling. Your heart jumps. Has the heat affected your eyesight? 'What is such a famous actor doing at Clifton?' you wonder. 'And why is he talking to John and Eva?'

Do you ...

| 1 | go and introduce yourself? | ▶ section 155 |
| 2 | wave at them as you walk past? | ▶ section 156 |

Chapter 8

155) Section 155

You feel very excited. 'Hello!' you say. 'Ryan Gosling? I can't believe it's you! It's an honour to meet you.'

Eva and John stop talking. They turn to look at you. You hold out your hand. Ryan Gosling takes your hand and shakes it slowly, laughing, 'Very good! That's very funny!' Then they return to their conversation and ignore* you. You don't know what to say or think. You walk to your office feeling embarrassed*.

A few minutes later, John Miller walks in. 'That was the actor who's come in for the Avoca ad.'

'What do you mean? That was Ryan Gosling! Is he going to be in the ad?'

'You're not listening,' says John. 'That isn't Ryan Gosling. He's just a voice-over* actor, he's here for a meeting about the Avoca ad. He looks similar to Ryan Gosling, that's all.'

'Really? I feel so embarrassed! I thought it was the real Ryan Gosling!'

'Don't be ridiculous*!' laughs John.

156) Section 156

You hold your breath and walk towards them, waving as you walk past. You run through the entrance door, to your office. You are still recovering from the excitement when Layla walks into your office. 'Hey!' you say. 'Have you seen Ryan Gosling yet? He's in reception.'

'Ha, ha.'

'No, seriously, I've just seen Ryan Gosling in reception. He was talking to Eva and John. Can you believe it?'

'What?'

Layla runs into the corridor and bumps into* Sylvia who is coming in the opposite direction.

'Ryan …?' begins Layla.

'I know!' screams Sylvia.

They both run in the direction of reception. You follow them.

Chapter 8

Section 157

You leave your phone and wallet at the side of the pool and dive in. You grab* Dagmar, who growls* and tries to bite you, but you hold on to her and swim to the edge of the pool. You give her to Hans, who dries her with a towel.

'My hero!' says Hans as he helps you out of the pool.

'Thanks!' you say. 'It's lucky I can swim!'

'I'm a great swimmer,' says Hans. 'But you looked so keen* to get into the pool, I didn't want to stop you!' He laughs.

You go to your room to get changed.

 section 161

Section 158

The next day, you wake up and you hear rain on the window. 'Rain?' you think. 'In the Australian desert?' Unfortunately, it is true. There is a terrible storm. As you open the window, you see raindrops hitting the dry streets of Alice Springs. Lightning flashes behind the mountains in the distance.

At breakfast, the location scout gives you the bad news. 'I'm sorry, but we can't look at the locations today. It's impossible to drive in this rain.'

'But we're going back to Sydney this evening!' you say.

'I'm sorry,' says the scout, 'but there's nothing we can do.'

Yesterday, you wasted* a day in the hotel and now you can't do the work. Without looking at the locations, you can't make your ad.

Your trip has been an expensive disaster!

Go back to the start of the chapter and try again. section 154

Section 159

'I must apologise, Mr Gosling. We're all quite excited to see you here,' says Layla.

'There's been some kind of misunderstanding,' Ryan Gosling starts.

'Oh, Mr Gosling, I expected you to have a Canadian accent! Have you picked up the Australian accent so soon?' Layla laughs.

Chapter 8

'Like I was saying, there's been some kind of misunderstanding. I'm not Ryan Gosling. Some people think I look like Ryan Gosling, that's all!'

Everyone in the room is silent.

160 Section 160

You find some cheese in the restaurant and take it back to the edge of the pool. 'Here, Dagmar!' you say. 'Cheesy, cheesy, here Dagmar! Come on girl.' Dagmar comes closer to you and you reach to grab* her, but your foot slips and you fall head-first into the pool. You wipe the water from your eyes. Hans collects Dagmar from the edge of the pool.

You get out of the pool. Your phone is wet and doesn't work. You go to your room to get changed. 'What will I do with Dagmar when we're making the film?' you ask yourself. 'It's going to be a real nightmare*!'

161 Section 161

The scout tells you about some very dramatic and exciting locations*, and you spend an hour in the hotel looking at the storyboard images and discussing how and where the Arrow can drive, where it can jump over rocks and do the other stunts* from the storyboard images. Then you go out to look at the locations in a four-wheel drive.

The car bumps over the rocky tracks and after about 15 minutes, just as you are arriving at the first location, Dagmar is sick. 'She gets car-sick* sometimes in Germany,' says Hans. 'I'm sorry about the car.' The car smells of sick all day and you have to drive with the windows open because of the smell. In 45°C heat, driving without air con is not pleasant, so Dagmar is not popular with you, Eva or the location scout.

162 Section 162

The following afternoon at 1.45, you are in the boardroom* checking the agenda* for the team meeting.

By 2.00 everyone is there. 'OK, item one is schedules*, so let's start with the TV ad. Have we booked the voice-over actor yet?'

90

Chapter 8

'Ryan Gosling?' says Sylvia and they all laugh. 'Yes, the voice-over actor is booked for 26th July.'

'Thanks. Film production?'

'We're still discussing technical issues, but the dates are fine,' says Eva. 'We're filming* on location* on the 12th–17th July, which are the dates we agreed with you and Hans.'

'Oh, I forgot. Is it OK if Dagmar comes?' you ask.

Eva sighs, 'I suppose so,' she says reluctantly*. 'If that's what the client wants. But it's incredibly important that you keep that dog under control. The last thing we need is Dagmar causing problems. Delays cost money and we'll have a big problem if we can't finish all the filming in time.'

'Understood,' you say. 'And Hans wants Dagmar to come when we check locations next week too.'

'Honestly! Can't that man go *anywhere* without his silly little dog?' asks Eva.

'I know it's a bit awkward*, but yes, he does travel everywhere with Dagmar.'

'Well, keep the dog away from anything breakable! What dates did we agree for that trip?'

'I have a note from the last meeting,' says Sylvia. 'We said ... the 20th and 21st of June.'

'Yes, that's what I have,' you agree. 'Can you book* tickets please, Sylvia?'

'Yes. Who's going?'

'Me, Hans, Eva and ...'

'... and Dagmar!' laughs Eva. 'Don't forget Dagmar!'

'I bet Hans wants Dagmar to fly in business class!' says John.

'Listen,' says Eva, 'I don't think we can do this on our own. We need some help with Dagmar – seriously.'

'Good idea,' you agree. 'Who should we take?'

'Me!' shouts Layla.

'I'm free on the 20th and 21st of June,' says Sylvia. 'My son's with his grandparents that week.'

Chapter 8

'It should be me who goes,' says John. 'I'm an account director. PR with clients is my job!'

'You choose,' says Eva. 'Hans and Dagmar are your responsibility.'

163 Section 163

A week later, you are on a Qantas flight from Sydney to Alice Springs. You are sitting next to Hans in business class. John and Eva are in economy seats at the back of the plane. It is a three-hour flight, so you and Hans have time to read and relax.

You land at 12.30 p.m. and the location scout meets you all and takes you to your hotel. During lunch, he explains, 'There's no rush. There are just seven locations to look at and we only need to choose two of them. They're all less than fifteen minutes from Alice Springs. To be honest, there are hundreds of brilliant locations around here – the landscape* is just spectacular*! We'll be able to see all of the locations in a day.'

'I'm quite tired,' says John. 'We're here all day tomorrow. Why don't we have the afternoon off and look around town?'

Eva looks up. 'The forecast* is cloud for tomorrow. I'd quite like to see some of the locations in good light.'

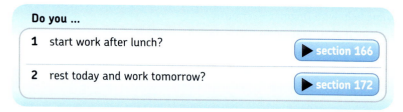

92

Chapter 8

Section 164

164

A week later, you are standing next to Hans and Eva in the departure lounge at Sydney Airport. The gate for the Alice Springs flight is about to close, but Layla hasn't checked in yet. She isn't answering her phone and she hasn't replied to your texts. You don't know what to do. There is nothing you can do, in fact. As you are walking onto the plane, your phone rings.

'It's me!' shouts Layla. 'I'm really sorry. I got the wrong day. I've come to work instead of to the airport – I forgot! I'll get the next flight. I'll pay for it myself!'

'The next flight's tomorrow, Layla. There are no more flights today.'

'OK,' she says, in a panic. 'I'll come tomorrow!'

'No,' you say. 'It's too late. We're coming back tomorrow. Our flight's leaving now so I must go. Goodbye.'

You and Eva sit next to Hans in business class. You land at 12.30 p.m. and the location scout takes you to your hotel. During lunch, he explains, 'There are just seven locations to look at and we only need to choose two of them. They're all less than 15 minutes from Alice Springs. To be honest, there are hundreds of brilliant locations near here – the landscape* is just spectacular*!'

Section 165

165

A week later, you are on a Qantas flight from Sydney to Alice Springs. You are sitting next to Hans in business class. Sylvia is in economy class at the back of the plane. It is a three-hour flight, so you and Hans have time to read and relax.

You land at 12.30 p.m. and the location scout takes you to your hotel. During lunch, he explains, 'There are just seven locations to look at and we only need to choose two of them. They're all less than fifteen minutes from here, so we can probably see them all this afternoon.'

Section 166

166

'I think that is a good idea,' says the scout. 'There isn't much to see in town! You need a car to get out of town to see anything interesting.'

93

Chapter 8

167 Section 167

⭐ You win 1 bonus point. Mark the scorecard on page 186.

You turn around and see Sylvia walking towards you. 'What's wrong?' she asks.

'It's Dagmar,' you say. 'She's in the pool.'

'Oh, don't worry,' says Sylvia. 'Dogs can swim. Look!' She walks round to the steps at the side of the pool. She makes some noises and Dagmar starts swimming towards her. When the dog is near the steps, Sylvia lifts* her out of the water. She wraps* the dog in a towel without getting any of her clothes wet. Suddenly, Hans comes out and he sees what has happened.

'My hero!' says Hans to Sylvia.

'Thanks!' she smiles.

Sylvia has saved the situation. It was a good idea to ask her to come with you.

'I'm glad* you're here!' you say to Sylvia. 'Can you look after Dagmar this afternoon while Hans and I go out with the scout?'

'No problem,' says Sylvia.

▶ section 173

168 Section 168

Away from the main highway*, the roads are rough tracks* and there are no signs. It is exciting because it feels like driving in the desert.

Chapter 8

The most important location is for the driving and jumping parts of the ad. For this you choose a hill* near Alice Springs. It is about 50 metres high and there is a rough track that the car can drive on at the bottom of the hill. The earth is an incredible dark-orange colour, and the landscape is covered with yellow rocks and small green trees. There are lots of kangaroos in the area, so you have to drive carefully.

The second location is very pretty. It is a spring, where water comes out of the ground. There are tall eucalyptus trees on each side of the water. One bank is grassy and the other is sandy, a bit like a beach. In the TV ad, the car is going to drive through the water very fast.

Section 169

169

Suddenly, there is a sound of barking* outside, then a loud splash. You run outside to see Dagmar in the hotel swimming pool. One of the staff* is trying to get her out with a long wooden pole. She is swimming slowly in a circle and her head keeps going under the water.

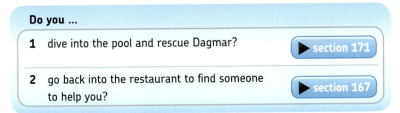

Do you ...

1 dive into the pool and rescue Dagmar? ▶ section 171

2 go back into the restaurant to find someone to help you? ▶ section 167

Section 170

170

Suddenly, there is a sound of barking* outside, then a loud splash. You run outside to see Dagmar swimming in the hotel swimming pool. One of the staff* is trying to get her out with a long wooden pole. She is swimming slowly in a circle and her head keeps going under the water.

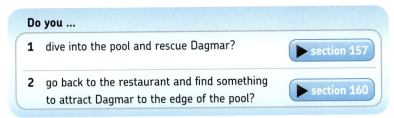

Do you ...

1 dive into the pool and rescue Dagmar? ▶ section 157

2 go back to the restaurant and find something to attract Dagmar to the edge of the pool? ▶ section 160

Chapter 8

171 Section 171

You put your phone and wallet on a chair and dive into the pool. You grab* Dagmar who growls* and tries to bite you, but you hold on to her and swim to the edge of the pool. You make a lot of noise and Hans and Sylvia come out to help you.

   Hans rushes* to help Dagmar. 'My hero!' he says. 'Thank you so much.'
   'It's OK,' you say. 'I saw she was in trouble so I had to save her.'
   'Well, I really appreciate* it,' says Hans.
   Sylvia hands you a towel. 'Here you are,' she says.
   'Thanks, Sylvia,' you say. 'Can you look after Dagmar this afternoon while Hans and I go out with the scout?'
   'No problem,' she says. 'Leave the dog with me and then you can concentrate on looking at the locations.' You go to your room to get changed.

172 Section 172

'I think that's a good idea,' says the scout. 'It's very hot today. Tomorrow might be cooler. The light will be fine. And there isn't much to see in town!' he laughs.

   You, Eva and Hans go inside the hotel to rest, while John sunbathes* by the swimming pool. When you meet for dinner, you hardly recognise* John. His face is bright red and fatter, like a tomato. 'I feel sick,' he explains.

   'You've got sunstroke*,' says the location scout. 'Too much sun. You've burnt your face. Go and have a cold bath, we'll get the doctor.'

   John goes back to his room. The doctor tells him to stay indoors for a day while he recovers. He can't help you with Dagmar at all.

173 Section 173

The scout tells you about some of the locations. You spend an hour in the hotel looking at the storyboard images and discussing how and where the Arrow can drive, where it can jump over rocks and do the other stunts*. Then you go out in a four-wheel drive to look at the locations.

Chapter 9

Section 174

It is the first day of filming* for the Avoca Arrow TV ad. You drive with Hans, John and Eva to the first location* near Alice Springs. There are about twenty people there when you arrive, all part of the film production crew*. There is also the special driver who is going to do all the dangerous scenes in the car, the stunt* driver, Steve Freeman.

There is a small tent where they are serving coffee and snacks*, so you offer to get a coffee for Hans. When you get back, Hans has gone. John is with Dagmar, holding her lead. 'Where's Hans?' you ask. John points at the car. Hans is getting into the passenger seat and Steve, the stunt driver, is getting in the driver's side. 'What's happening?' you ask.

'You see the guy with the leather jacket? He's the stunt driver. He invited Hans to go for a test-drive,' explains John.

Eva sees you. 'Your client* is already causing problems!' she complains*. 'We're about to film the first scene, but now the stunt driver is taking Hans for a drive! This is exactly the sort of thing you're supposed to stop!'

'The stunt driver insisted,' John tells you. 'And Hans was very excited, so I said it would be OK if they were quick.'

'But there isn't time for this,' you say. 'We're waiting to start filming. And it might be dangerous. We don't want anything to happen to Hans!'

You hear the loud sound of an engine, and you look up to see the car driving slowly down the hill*.

Chapter 9

> **Do you ...**
> 1 try and stop them? There isn't time and it might be dangerous.
> 2 let them go? It is only two minutes and Hans wants to go.

175 Section 175

 You win 1 bonus point. Mark the scorecard on page 186.
'Hi, you must be Steve Freeman,' you say, and you introduce yourself.
  'It's good to meet you,' says Steve. 'Hans is a real character! I like him.'
  'Yes, he's enthusiastic. I was worried when you took him out though. Is it dangerous out there?'
  'Dangerous? No! Not if you know what you're doing.'
  'Er, so do you think Hans will be OK? Now he's on his own.'
  'He'll be fine. He saw what I did. He can just copy me. And anyway, we can watch him from up here,' he explains. 'John asked me to make sure that Hans was happy, so I gave him a ride.'
  You chat to Steve for five minutes. He is friendly and funny, he tells some brilliant jokes. 'If you ever need anything,' says Steve, 'call my company "Steve's stunts". My extension number is 288.'

   Go to the Contacts section on page 186 and write down Steve's extension.

176 Section 176

'I'm sorry Eva, but there's nothing I can do. I promise I'll stop Hans causing any more problems – John, perhaps you can be a bit more helpful too.'
  'I've got Dagmar,' he laughs. 'That's an important job! Anyway, it'll only be two minutes.'
  'Never mind the time – it might be dangerous!' says Eva. 'We haven't got insurance* for Hans to go in the car!'
  There is a loud roar* as the car drives away very quickly. The wheels spin and a big cloud of red dust flies into the air.

Chapter 9

Section 177

177

Ten minutes later, Eva and the director are talking. The director is looking at his watch and shaking* his head. You can hear the sound of the car in the distance and it seems to be getting closer.

'They're going so fast!' says one of the crew. As the car comes up a track* along the side of the hill, it goes over a bump and flies through the air for a few seconds. You close your eyes and wait for the crash, but when you open your eyes again, the car is back on the track.

'Yeah!' shout the crew. 'Nice jump!' A few of the crew members clap*. You are beginning to get very worried. When the car is just a few hundred metres away, it turns very quickly to avoid* some rocks and it starts to spin in circles. The car disappears into a huge* cloud of red dust and you can't hear the engine any more.

'Oh, no! What's happened?' you ask.

Section 178

178

The dust blows away and you can see the car on the side of the track. Steve Freeman gets out of the car to look at it from a few different angles. Then, he gets back inside and reverses* the car back onto the track and then races up the hill to where you are.

'Poor Hans,' you say to John. 'He's probably terrified!'

You run over to the car to help Hans out. But Hans is laughing loudly and shouting, 'More! More! That was brilliant!'

Steve gets out of the car and says to Hans, 'You drive, mate*!'

'Me?' asks Hans.

'Yeah, go for it, just follow the same route we took,' Steve says.

'No!' shout you and Eva together. But before you can reach the car, Hans has moved over to the driver's seat and started to drive away. You hear an excited scream as he waves his hand out of the window and the car flies down the hill again.

Eva looks at you angrily. 'You can't let this happen. Do something!'

99

Chapter 9

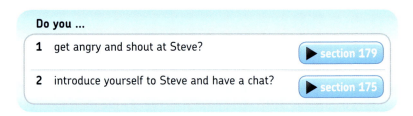

179 Section 179

'That was really dangerous and really stupid!' you shout at the stunt driver. Steve looks at you. He puts his hands on his hips and he doesn't say anything. 'I can't believe you did that!' you say. Steve's eyes get narrower. He continues to look at you, but he doesn't say anything. 'Can't you speak?' you ask.

'Sure, I can speak. Don't you have any manners*?' he asks.

'Manners? Manners? You nearly killed my most important client and you think I should be polite!'

'Listen,' Steve says. 'John asked me to make sure that Hans was happy. He wanted to go for a ride so I said yes. I did it to help you guys,' he explains.

'But where is he now? He's driving around in your car on his own!'

'First, that isn't my car — it's your car. Second, I was just being nice to him. It's your job to look after him.'

You seem to have made an enemy.

180 Section 180

You run after the car. When you are next to the driver's window, you shout, 'Hans! Hans! Stop, there isn't time for this. We need to start filming.'

'Get out of the way!' shouts Hans. Then he says to the stunt driver, 'Drive!' The driver looks at you, but Hans says, 'You said two minutes. Let's go!'

'But we haven't got insurance* for you to go in the car!' you shout. 'It might be dangerous!'

'This is my ad. Leave us alone!' shouts Hans, angrily. Then he turns to the driver and says, 'Come on! Let's go!' The engine roars* loudly and the wheels spin in the sand. You are instantly covered in red dust as the car

100

drives away very quickly. There is sand in your mouth and eyes and ears. Hans is already causing problems. You turn around and the production crew start to laugh and clap*. Everyone is laughing and shouting – everyone except Eva. You go to wash your face and hands.

Section 181

Hans has been gone for five minutes now and you can hear the car on the other side of the hill. Suddenly, the sound of the engine gets much louder. You can't actually see the car yet, all you can see is a cloud of red dust moving towards you.

In the other direction, you notice something much bigger moving towards the track, followed by a cloud of dust. 'What's that?' you ask the location scout*.

'Camels. They were brought here over 100 years ago to transport things in the outback. When they stopped using them, a few hundred were left here. Now, there are about 750,000!'

'Are they dangerous?'

'They drink all the water, so they aren't popular with farmers. They break fences and they can really damage a car if you crash into one.'

You look at the camels. You can now see that they are running towards the track at the bottom of the hill. Hans could crash into the camels and have a serious accident. You need to do something to stop Hans or the camels. John is standing next to you.

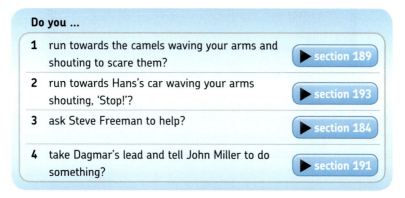

Chapter 9

182 Section 182

Look at the Contacts section on page 186.

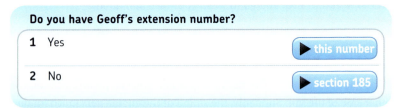

183 Section 183

You talk with the actor playing the nephew for a few minutes. Then you meet the uncle, who is just as you had imagined – 30-something with slightly grey hair at the sides and a warm smile. The two actors represent both ends of the age-group that the car is aimed* at. You and Hans have a busy day watching the filming and then approving* the results. All the time you stay in contact with John about the situation with Dagmar.

You take Hans for dinner in Manly to celebrate the end of a busy and successful week. After a while, you mention Dagmar. 'I'm glad John is with her,' Hans says. 'He's very kind. Hey, cheers!' Your glasses clink. 'I'm very happy with this film!' he continues. 'This ad's going to be sensational!'

Chapter 9

Section 184

184

Steve takes out a gun. You are shocked* and you react immediately. 'No!' you shout.

'Trust me,' he says. 'I know what I'm doing.'

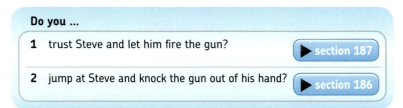

Section 185

185

The next day, you and the crew drive to the fresh water spring. This is the location for the next part of the advert. The plan is for the car to drive through the water at high speed. Steve puts on some swimming trunks and walks through the water with a long stick. Then, he drives slowly through the water to practise the route. Finally, he drives through fast, and water splashes high into the air.

Hans is very excited and while the crew are setting up the cameras, he takes the car and drives it fast through the water. BANG! There is a loud crashing noise and the car stops suddenly in the middle of the water. The air bags have inflated and all you can see is one of Hans's arms, waving. The car starts to fill up with water, so you have to run into the spring with John to pull Hans out of a window.

'What happened?' Hans asks.

'Rocks,' says Steve. 'I checked where there are rocks under the water and where the deep parts are. Hans didn't know where the rocks were.' The car has filled up with water. The crew can't move it, so they call a truck from a garage in Alice Springs to pull the car out of the water.

Fortunately, you have a spare Avoca Arrow and the film crew spend a few hours filming Steve drive through the water. Hans is unusually quiet and stays in the tent drinking coffee and eating snacks.

103

Chapter 9

186 Section 186

You jump at Steve and knock the gun out of his hand. 'What did you do that for?' he asks.

'The gun!' you say. 'I thought–' Your sentence is cut off by the sound of the camels running into the car. After about a minute the dust disappears. The car looks destroyed and you can't see Hans moving.

'I thought you were going to shoot the gun, and I didn't want you to injure Hans!'

'That was stupid! This isn't a real gun. It's a starter pistol, it's used for starting races. It makes a really loud sound and I wanted it to scare the camels so they would run away from the car. Now look what's happened!'

A first aid medic shouts from a Land Rover, 'Get in!'

You drive down the hill to the Arrow. Hans has blood on his face and a cut on his forehead, but he says he feels fine. The medic examines* him and calls an ambulance. Hans needs to go to hospital to check he is OK. The car is ruined*.

The filming must stop and Hans has to stay in hospital for two weeks.

Go back to the start of the chapter and try again.

187 Section 187

The camels have almost reached the track. Steve Freeman lifts the gun up and fires it into the air three times. The camels immediately turn and start to run in the opposite direction. Hans's car drives up the track a few seconds later. You feel very relieved* and you smile at Steve.

'Well done! I was scared when you got out your gun, but I'm glad* I trusted you! Thank you,' you say.

'No worries,' says Steve. 'And by the way, this isn't a real gun! It's just a starter pistol for starting races.'

Hans gets out of the car. 'Have you had a good time, Hans?' you ask.

'Fantastic!' he laughs.

'Great. I have to ask you a favour. Can you stay with me today? The director wants to start filming now and we don't want to run over schedule*. Please don't disappear again!'

Chapter 9

Section 188

188

The director and the crew have a meeting with Steve Freeman and Eva Campano. Steve drives along the course quite slowly while the crew move their cameras to the best positions. They test the angles about ten times and then the director says, 'Great work everyone. Lunch for 30 minutes, then we start filming.'

After lunch, the filming starts. Steve gets into the Avoca Arrow. He drives down the hill and along the bottom of the valley. He is going very fast, much faster than with Hans. It looks like a scene from an action movie. The car jumps over some rocks. 'Great!' says the director. 'Let's go again.' Steve goes back to the start and repeats the stunt several times. Steve is a very experienced driver and he knows how to drive the car at its limits.

At about 3.00, the director says, 'I think we have what we need here. Give us an hour to check the film and we'll show you.'

While Hans and Steve are looking at the engine of the Arrow, you and John take Dagmar for a walk. 'We really need to work together on this,' you say. 'Hans is a difficult person to manage and we won't survive the week unless we cooperate*.'

'I completely agree,' says John.

By the time you get back, Hans has approved* all the short clips of film. The day has been a success. The crew clear up the site and you all drive back to Alice Springs.

Section 189

189

You run down the hill towards the camels, waving* your arms in the air and shouting. There are a lot of camels and they aren't afraid of you. Some of the camels change direction. Now they are running towards you!

Hans uses the horn in the car to make a loud sound to scare the animals, but it doesn't help. The camels are much faster than you and you are suddenly surrounded by them. You can't see anything except the heads, necks and bodies of the large animals. Then a very big leg comes towards your head. There is no time to move. Everything goes black.

Some days later, you wake up in hospital in Alice Springs. The doctors tell you that you have serious injuries and you need several months to

105

Chapter 9

recover. Your colleagues from Clifton come to see you and Hans sends a card and some flowers.

For now, your advertising career* is over.

Go back to the start of the chapter and try again.

190 Section 190

The next day you film the scene with the crocodile fight. Geoff from Technix arrives with an enormous* model crocodile. It is very heavy and you help him carry it to the edge of the spring, but once it is in the water it floats and is easy to move around. The actor who plays the nephew in the ad gets into the water too. The director gives him some instructions, and he starts to roll and jump, fighting the model crocodile. Dagmar starts to bark*. She is making so much noise that you and John move her a few hundred metres away, to some shade*.

The crew* film the fighting from a few different angles. It is funny to watch the actor splashing and fighting with the crocodile and you can hear Hans laughing.

'It looks great,' you say to John. Just then, Dagmar escapes and starts running back to the spring. 'I thought you had her,' you say.

'And I thought you had her,' he replies.

Dagmar is barking loudly and runs into the water. He jumps at the actor and the crocodile and they all fall under the water in a big splash.

'My actor!' says the director.

'My model crocodile!' says Geoff.

'My little dog!' says Hans.

You look at John and try not to laugh. You are getting used to all the problems that Hans and Dagmar are causing. One of the crew pulls Dagmar out of the water and gives her to Hans. The actor stands up. He is injured. A doctor treats his cut at the edge of the spring. 'It's not serious,' he says, 'but you can't get water in this cut. No more filming today.'

The director and the film crew are angry about the actor's injury and about the change to the film. Now the ad won't have a crocodile. You think Hans will be angry too because he really wanted the scene with the crocodile fight, but he is more worried about Dagmar. 'I hope she doesn't catch a cold,' he says.

Chapter 9

You thank Geoff for his help with the model crocodile and apologise* for what happened with Dagmar, but secretly you are pleased. You think the ad will be better without the crocodile.

Section 191

191

'John, quick. Do something!' you shout. John looks at you, in panic.

'The camels!' you shout. John looks left and right but he doesn't move.

It is too late. The camels run in front of the car and Hans turns to avoid them. He crashes into a tree and there is a very loud bang. You run down the hill to the car and help Hans to get out.

'What …?' he asks. 'What …?'

'Camels,' you explain. 'Wild camels.'

'Camels?' asks Hans. 'Are we in Egypt?'

A medic arrives. He looks into Hans's eyes with a torch* and he checks his blood pressure. Hans sits down. Then he closes his eyes as he lies down, very quickly.

'Why is he sleeping?' you ask. 'Is he in shock?'

'He isn't sleeping. He's unconscious. We need to get him to hospital.'

The filming must stop and Hans is seriously injured.

Go back to the start of the chapter and try again.

Section 192

192

You have three more days of filming in Alice Springs. It all goes very well. John looks after Dagmar while you look after Hans, making sure he doesn't get in the way of the film production. At the end of the fifth day, you and the crew fly back to Sydney to film the parts of the ad where the car is at the uncle's house.

The following morning, you arrive at an address in north Sydney with John, Hans and Eva. The film production crew are already there with their cameras and a mini train track along the side of

Chapter 9

the road. It is Saturday and the road is closed while they are filming. You all get out of the car, and Dagmar jumps out after Hans. She runs to the mini train track just as the camera is travelling along the track. It hits Dagmar and she makes a terrible* sound.

John and Hans comfort Dagmar. She looks OK, but she is making a lot of noise. Hans is very worried, but he can't take Dagmar to the vet's* because it would be too expensive to stop the filming for a few hours. John says, 'I'll take her to the vet's in Manly. It's only five minutes by car. You stay here, Hans.'

'Yes, thanks John,' you say. Hans looks very worried. 'I'm sure Dagmar will be OK, but it's better to be safe than sorry. John will look after her.'

193 Section 193

You run down the hill towards Hans, waving* your arms in the air and shouting, 'Stop! Stop!' Hans looks at you and waves back, smiling. He isn't looking where he is going. Suddenly, the camels run across the track. A few of them run into the car and there is a loud noise.

When you get to the car, Hans is very angry with you. 'Why were you waving at me? You distracted me and I didn't see the camels!'

'I was trying to warn* you,' you say.

'This is all your fault!' he shouts. 'I've hurt my neck.'

A medic arrives, running with a first aid bag. He examines* Hans and calls the air ambulance. Hans has injured his neck and he needs to go to hospital.

The filming must stop and Hans blames you for everything.

Go back to the start of the chapter and try again.

Chapter 10

Section 194

It is the night of the ANZA Awards. The ANZAs are the Australia and New Zealand Advertising Awards, and they are one of the biggest awards in the industry. You are going to the ceremony because the Avoca Arrow advert has been a huge* success! It is now four months since you recorded the advert in the outback. Since then, it has appeared on TV and online. Journalists have written several stories about it and talked about what a great ad it was.

It is now 8.00 p.m. and you are sitting with your colleagues in a limousine* on your way to the ceremony. Your boss, Karen, is happy and laughing. John Miller is wearing a tuxedo* that he must have bought a few years ago. It is now a little too small for him, but he is in a really good mood*. The only nervous person is Eva Campano. Eva keeps taking a small mirror out of her bag and checking her hair. Her phone is buzzing all the time and she is receiving hundreds of messages from her friends and colleagues*. For a creative director, an ad industry award is the highest honour in their career. An ANZA is more important for her than for anyone else in the company.

When you arrive at the ceremony, you get out of the limousine. Cameras flash from all directions

Although Clifton have their own table, your colleagues have many friends and contacts in the industry. John, Eva and Karen soon see people

Chapter 10

that they know. They all move to different parts of the room and start networking*. Suddenly, you are alone in a room full of people.

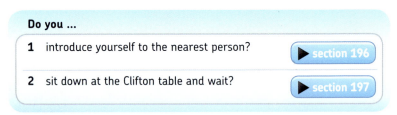

195 Section 195

'Why didn't you mention us?' you ask. You look at John Miller for support*, but he looks surprised and doesn't say anything.

'I thanked the whole team,' says Karen.

'You didn't thank us by name,' you say.

'This is an award for the agency and for the creative director,' says Karen. 'Nobody thanks the account directors in moments like these.'

'Perhaps you don't know what we do for the company,' you say.

'What you do?' says Eva. 'It's the creative team that keeps this company in business. You just have lunch with clients. We do all the work.'

'I don't believe this!' you shout. 'We worked for that award too.'

'Shhh!' says Karen. 'People are listening. We'll talk about this next week at work.'

You want to argue* more, but you decide to keep quiet. You don't enjoy the evening and everyone on the Clifton table looks unhappy.

Next week, when you get to work, Karen asks to see you in her office. 'Thank you for your work on Avoca,' she says, 'but I don't think the team is working anymore.'

'What do you mean?' you ask.

'The creative team aren't happy with you, and you insulted Eva and me, at the dinner. I'll write you a very positive reference* for your next job.'

'I ... I don't understand.'

'I'm sorry but your behaviour at the awards ceremony was not acceptable.' says Karen. She looks you in the eye. 'It's time for you to seek* employment elsewhere.'

She has sacked* you!

Go back to the start of the chapter and try again.

Chapter 10

Section 196

196

The person next to you is a lady wearing a dark blue dress. She has a very expensive necklace*, made of emeralds. She has long red hair and freckles. When you turn round to her, she smiles. 'Excuse me,' you say, 'Can I introduce myself?' You say your name, and you add, 'Pleased to meet you.' You give the woman your hand.

She looks puzzled*, but she smiles. 'Susannah Avoca,' she says.

What do you say?

1 'What are you doing here at the ANZA Awards?' ▶ section 200

2 'It's nice to see you here.' ▶ section 201

Section 197

197

There are several seats at the table. You choose one and sit down. For about ten minutes, nobody speaks to you. Then a hand appears on your left. The chair moves and a man sits next to you. He has a very white face and curly hair.

'Is your name "Clifton"?' He asks. Then he laughs. 'Ha, ha, ha. Can I sit here?'

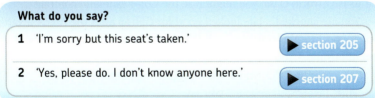

What do you say?

1 'I'm sorry but this seat's taken.' ▶ section 205

2 'Yes, please do. I don't know anyone here.' ▶ section 207

111

Chapter 10

198 Section 198

After the awards ceremony, you have a free weekend, so you can relax. Your friend Pete Deng is in Sydney and he invites you to a barbeque at his sister's house. She lives by the coast so her home has wonderful views over the sea. It is a sunny day with a few clouds in the sky. The sea is rough and there are surfers out on the waves. It feels good to breath the fresh sea air after so many days in air-conditioned offices. You and Pete are doing the cooking. Pete starts chatting about business. 'Congratulations on your ANZA award,' he says. 'You guys did a great job on the Avoca Arrow.'

'Thanks,' you say. 'Let's hope we can do the same for tourism in Gondwanaland.'

'Right,' says Pete. 'Actually, I wanted to have a chat about that – off the record*, just you and me.'

Pete starts talking very quietly. It is a hot day, but you suddenly feel very cold.

199 Section 199

'Is something wrong?' you ask. 'Gondwanaland is a very important client for us.'

'I know that, but things are changing,' says Pete.

'What's wrong?'

'We're thinking of changing our advertising agency.'

'What?' You ask.

'It's not my decision. It's my boss, Anastasia. Another advertising agency has offered the Tourism Board a new deal. We're happy with Clifton's work, but Anastasia's considering this offer. If Clifton's new advertising campaign* for us isn't world class, you might lose the Gondwanaland contract*.'

You are shocked*. Life looked good for Clifton after the ANZA award, but if you lose the contract with Gondwanaland, your company will go out of business. You have to save that contract.

'We never had this conversation, right?' says Pete.

'Fine. I won't tell anyone,' you say.

'I want you to succeed, but Anastasia is my boss and she makes all the decisions. I'm just a gopher.'

'I understand.'

Chapter 10

'There's one more thing,' says Pete. 'This next advertising campaign is going to be the hardest one yet.'

'Why's that?'

'Haven't you seen this morning's newspapers?' asks Pete. 'Have a look. Then you'll see what the problem is.'

 section 214

Section 200

'What am I doing here?' asks Susannah. 'I'm hoping to collect the award for our car ad. You do advertise our car, don't you?'

'Do we?' you ask.

'Of course you do! You work with our brand* manager Hans Fischer!'

Suddenly you realise your mistake*. Her name is Susannah Avoca – she must be part of the Avoca family. They own Avoca Autos. This is one of your biggest clients* and you didn't recognise her.

Do you ...

1 pretend that you have met Susannah before? ▶ section 202

2 talk about Hans? ▶ section 208

Section 201

'It was very nice of your company to invite us to the awards,' says Susannah. 'We're so pleased with all the work that Clifton did on the Avoca Arrow.'

Of course! You suddenly realise that Susannah is a member of the Avoca family. They own Avoca Autos. Sylvia forgot to tell you that Susannah Avoca had been invited to the ceremony. The others join you and you introduce them to Susannah. Karen and Susannah know each other very well and they start chatting. You sit down at your table.

The ceremony is about to begin!

 section 204

Section 202

'Oh yes! Susannah! How nice to meet you again!'

'I don't believe we've ever met,' says Susannah. 'I've never met anyone from Clifton before, except for Karen Booth, obviously.'

Chapter 10

John Miller arrives with a drink in his hand. 'Who's your friend?' he asks, rather rudely.

'Er, John, this is Susannah Avoca, who runs Avoca Autos.'

John's face goes white. He didn't recognise* Susannah at all. 'I'm sorry ...' he says. 'P ... P ... Pleased to meet you, Ms Avoca.'

'Pleased to meet you too,' says Susannah coldly. She sees someone on the other side of the room and waves* to them. 'Please excuse me.'

When she leaves you, John and you look at each other. 'You could have warned* me,' says John.

'I didn't know who she was either.'

Fortunately, the person she meets is your boss Karen. They are chatting together and eventually* they sit at your table. Susannah Avoca sits as far away as possible from you and John.

The award ceremony is about to begin!

 section 204

203 Section 203

'Calm down?' shouts the man. 'You're asking me to calm down. All my life, I work under incredible pressure. My life isn't calm. How can I calm down? Do you understand me?' The man jumps up and knocks a glass of water over. You stand up because you don't want your clothes to get wet. The man is waving* his arms around. He is speaking so fast that you don't understand him.

Suddenly, you feel a strong hand on your elbow. The security guards are next to you and the man. 'Please come with us,' they say.

'I'm not with him!' you say. Unfortunately, Daniel is shouting a lot and he is fighting with the security guards. No one listens to you.

'This way.' The security guards take you both out of the ceremony in front of all your colleagues. The last thing you see is John Miller. He is watching you, open-mouthed.

Outside, you feel angry and embarrassed*. Daniel walks away. You are in a side street with rubbish bins. Someone calls you on your mobile phone. It is Karen. 'What were you doing?' she says. 'I've never been so embarrassed in my life!' She is furious*. Everyone at Clifton saw you, and photographers took your photo. 'This is the most important night in the company's history!' says Karen. 'Now it's a disaster.'

'I can explain–' you say.

'Don't bother,' says Karen. 'You can't work with our customers now. Everyone saw you.'

'What do you mean?'

'It's over,' says Karen. 'Don't come back to work.'

Clifton has sacked you!

Go back to the start of the chapter and try again.

Section 204

The presenter arrives on stage. He is a famous celebrity with blond hair, an amazing suntan* and teeth that are too white and perfect to be natural. 'Ladies and gentlemen! Copywriters and creatives, account directors and gophers, welcome to the 15th Australia and New Zealand Advertising Awards. These are the ANZAs!'

Everyone laughs when he says 'gophers', a slang* word for staff* who make the coffee and do the unimportant jobs in a company. The ceremony is entertaining, but very long, and your category is the last one. Finally, the presenter has the envelope* in his hand. 'Now, it's time to announce the final award of the evening. The ANZA award for best cinema or television advertisement goes to ...' There is a pause. You don't breathe. You feel your heart pumping in your chest. The presenter can't open the envelope. He takes some more time.

'Come on, come on!' you think. You are getting impatient.

Finally, the presenter has the paper in his hand. 'The ANZA award for the best television or film advertisement goes to the Avoca Arrow advert by Clifton Creative Agency.'

Everyone cheers. The whole audience is clapping*. Karen and Eva are out of their seats. You stand up too, smiling. It is time to pick up the award, but Eva is looking at you and shaking her head 'no'.

Do you ...

1 join Eva and Karen and collect the award?   ▶ section 209

2 sit down and watch Eva and Karen?   ▶ section 210

Chapter 10

205 Section 205

'Taken?' the man says. 'What do you mean? There's no one here. Ha, ha, ha!'

'These are the seats for the people in my company,' you say.

'Your company?' the man says. 'Who cares? I want to sit here and nobody is going to stop me!'

'I'm sorry,' you say, 'but you can't sit there.'

'I said I wanted to sit here,' the man says aggressively. He pulls out the chair. 'Are you going to stop me?'

'Yes,' says a voice behind you. You and the man turn around.

206 Section 206

You are relieved* to see John Miller. He clearly recognises* the man at your table. 'Daniel, we've had this problem before,' says John. 'These seats are taken and it's time for you to go.' John stands with his arms folded. He looks very serious.

'John Miller,' Daniel says. 'What are you so angry about?'

'This is a big night for our company,' says John. 'We don't want to have an embarrassing argument. You know this isn't your table, so why don't you leave us alone?'

'I want to see my old colleagues,' says Daniel.

'They don't want to see you,' says John.

Daniel looks at the chair and then he looks at John. 'Yeah, well, I'll see you later John and ... Clifton,' he adds looking at you. He sniffs and walks away.

When the man has gone, John smiles at you. 'Don't worry about Daniel,' he says. 'He's a freelancer* and a great copywriter*, but he has bad moments. He worked for us a long time ago, but we had to ask him to leave the company.'

'Thank you for helping me,' you say.

'Ah it's no problem. I used to be a rugby player, you know. I'm not frightened of a situation like that.'

'Well, we're all on the same team now, John,' you say.

'That's right,' he agrees. 'We did a fantastic job on the Avoca Arrow. The company's future looks great now.'

Chapter 10

You both smile. The others join you, including a woman that you have never met before. Karen introduces her as Susannah Avoca, a member of the family who own Avoca Autos.

The ceremony is about to begin!

Section 207

The man sits down very quickly. You notice that his eyes are red and he looks like he doesn't get a lot of sleep. 'Daniel. Daniel Laight, that's my name.'

'Why are you here at the awards ceremony?' you ask very politely.

'What am I doing here? Ha ha ha.' Daniel starts speaking very fast. He sounds angry and unhappy. 'What am I doing here? That's a good question. I'm wasting* my life. I've worked in advertising for twenty years. Twenty years!' You want to say something, but it is impossible to interrupt Daniel. He is now speaking very loudly and other people are looking at you. 'I was going to be a writer, a novelist. The public just don't understand my work. Do you know the biggest problem? Do you? I'm a copywriter* and I'm under pressure all the time to produce great ideas. I gave my best story ideas for adverts that were selling socks and washing powder! I'm an artist and I sold all my great ideas. So what am I doing here? What ... am ... I ... doing ... here?' he finally shouts.

You are worried about the situation.

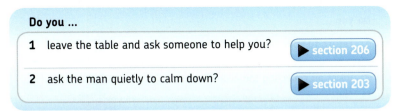

Section 208

⭐ You win 1 bonus point. Mark the scorecard on page 186.

'Ah, Hans! Of course,' you say. 'He goes everywhere with Dagmar.'

'I hate that dog,' says Susannah. 'We had to tell Hans to stop bringing it to meetings. I do apologise* if he's been taking her to your company too. I hope it won't bother you in future.'

117

Chapter 10

'No, Ms Avoca, Dagmar won't bother us in the future,' you say. 'Anyway, we're creative people in the advertising business so it was never a problem to have Dagmar in the meetings. Everything helps to give us ideas.'

'Oh, I'm pleased to hear that,' says Susannah. 'And of course, you've produced a fantastic ad for us. We're really hoping to win tonight.'

'Us too,' you say. You didn't recognise* Susannah in the beginning, but now you have saved an embarrassing situation. The others join you and you introduce them to Susannah. Karen and Susannah know each other very well and they start chatting. You sit down at your table.

The ceremony is about to begin!

209 Section 209

All three of you are standing on the stairs that lead to the stage. Above you, the presenter is holding your award. The audience is clapping*.

'What are you doing?' whispers Eva.

'*You* don't collect the award,' says Karen, 'the creative director and the head of account services collect it. That's us, not you.'

'I'm on the stairs,' you say, 'I can't go down again. It would look ridiculous*.'

'What shall we do?' asks Eva.

You all look around. The audience is still clapping. 'Don't be shy, Clifton!' says the presenter.

210 Section 210

You stay in your seat while Eva and Karen collect the award. Everyone is clapping* and Eva looks delighted*. In her speech*, Karen thanks her team, but she doesn't mention you, John, Layla or any of the other workers by name. When they return to their seats, they show you the award.

Chapter 10

'I'm so happy for you all,' Susannah Avoca says. 'The Avoca Arrow advert is the best one we've ever run.' Then she leaves you to speak to another business contact on the other side of the room.

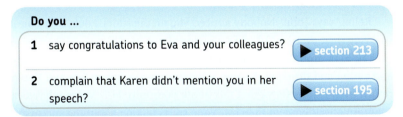

Section 211

'This is so embarrassing,' says Eva. Together you stand on the stage and Eva makes a speech*. You stand in the background*, feeling very uncomfortable. The award does not feel like an achievement* now. When you return to your seats, photographers come to your table. Karen and Eva can't complain* because they are smiling for their photos. Susannah Avoca also asks to look at the award.

In the limousine home, Karen finally speaks to you. 'In this business, the creative director accepts the award with the head of account services,' she says.

'That was my big moment!' complains Eva.

'I'm sorry, everyone' you say. 'Next time we win the biggest award in Australian advertising, I'll stay in my seat.' Everyone laughs.

'It's true,' says John Miller. 'Smile everyone. Today we're the number one team. Come on everyone. Let's celebrate!'

Now the party really begins. You don't get home until 4.00 a.m. but you are very happy with your night's work.

Section 212

As you return to your seat, you feel like everyone is watching you. You sit down and clap slowly while Eva and Karen take the award.

'What were you doing?' whispers John Miller.

'I thought the whole team collected the award,' you say.

Chapter 10

'No, it doesn't work like that,' says John. 'It's like the movies. You know, a film director accepts the award for best film, but lots of other people do the work too.'

'I feel so embarrassed*,' you say.

'Relax,' says John. 'Nobody noticed you on the stairs. Look, everyone's enjoying their dinner. Nobody's thinking about you.'

You look around the room. It's true. People are laughing and joking and eating and drinking. No one is looking at you. When Eva and Karen return to the table, they don't talk about your mistake*. Susannah Avoca congratulates them and then everyone starts talking about the successful advert.

John picks up the award. He inspects it like a father looking at his new baby. 'This is a fantastic day for Clifton,' he says. Then he turns to you. 'I had my doubts* about you in the beginning, but you've been a real success. We've done great work together. Come on, everybody let's celebrate a real triumph for Clifton!'

Now the party really begins. You don't get home until 4.00 a.m. but you are very happy with your night's work.

213 Section 213

'Congratulations on the award,' you say, hiding your disappointment.

'Thanks to both you and John as account directors' says Eva. 'It's nice to work with people who allow me to do my creative work.'

'Yes, thank you,' says Karen. 'In fact, I have some good news for you. I'm giving everyone on this table a $5,000 bonus. Excellent work everybody! Clifton is back in business.'

Everyone claps and smiles.

'You deserve it,' says Karen. 'With the Avoca contract and the Gondwanaland Tourism contract, the future is looking great for Clifton!'

Chapter 11

Section 214

MELBOURNE MORNING POST

Composer Dies in Stinger Horror
Red alert on beaches of Gondwanaland

The holiday resorts of Gondwanaland in northern Australia were rocked by the sudden death yesterday of composer Ambrosius Smith, 78. According to local police, Mr Smith arrived in Gondwanaland at about 5.00 p.m. yesterday after his successful series of concerts in Sydney and Tokyo. He decided to go for a short swim before dinner, when he touched a box jellyfish in the water. It is believed that Mr Smith of New York, USA died of a heart attack shortly after coming into contact with the animal.

As well as a tragedy for Mr Smith's family and music lovers everywhere, the attack sent a shockwave around the local community. The economy of Gondwanaland is almost completely dependent on tourism. The box jellyfish has never been seen in the area before. If the animals start appearing on local beaches, the tourism industry could collapse.

▶ section 215

Chapter 11

215 Section 215

The next day you arrive for work and Karen invites you into her office. It is raining and the water pours down the window behind her.

'I hate days like this,' Karen says. 'Tourists think it's always sunny in Australia, but we have some bad weather too. Of course, it's sunny in the tropical parts of the country – in Gondwanaland.'

'Yes,' you say, 'our biggest client*.'

'Have you ever been there?' asks Karen.

'No, never,' you say.

'It's beautiful. It's paradise on earth,' says Karen. 'But there's trouble in paradise. Have you seen the paper?'

'Yes, I know about the composer's death. It's horrible.'

'Tragic.' Karen shakes her head. 'The box jellyfish is the world's most venomous* animal. People die from stings* from time to time and it doesn't make the news. However, Ambrosius Smith was incredibly famous. This story's gone all around the world. The danger is that people associate Gondwanaland with danger and not with holidays.'

'Yes, I know,' you say.

'I spoke to Anastasia Dimitris this morning, she's the head of the Gondwanaland Tourism Board. She wants us to design a new advertising campaign* to rescue Gondwanaland. I'm putting you in charge of it. You're flying to see her on Wednesday and to visit the area. This is a very important job. Despite our success with Avoca, Clifton can't survive without the Gondwanaland contract*.'

'Leave it with me, Karen,' you say confidently. However, you don't feel confident*. The meeting ends. Thanks to the information from Pete, you know you have to impress Anastasia if you want to keep this client. You need to find out more about her.

Who do you talk to?	
1 Eva Campano	▶ section 227
2 John Miller	▶ section 217
3 Layla Evans	▶ section 231
4 Sylvia Watson	▶ section 234

Chapter 11

Section 216

There is a changing room on the boat so you quickly change into your swimming costume. You also decide it is time to tell the truth. You feel bad because the hotel receptionist will be in trouble with Nikos.

When you come out on the boat, you take the piece of paper. 'Look! Nikos, I've just found your note in my bag,' you lie. 'The hotel receptionist gave it to me, but I thought it was a bill* so I didn't read it.'

'Good,' says Nikos. 'I knew that I gave the note to the receptionist.'

'It's lucky you have your swimming things, anyway,' says Anastasia.

'Well, I'm very excited about our trip,' you say. 'Swimming in paradise!'

Section 217

John is sitting in the office that you both share*. He is looking at the screen on his smart phone. 'I hate these things,' he says. 'We're connected to work all the time. If you don't answer an email in five minutes, people get worried and they send you a message on the phone.'

'Er, yes, John,' you say. 'I need your help. I'm going to start working with Anastasia Dimitris.'

'Oh, Anastasia!' he says. 'She's impossible to work with. She never likes anything. I think we produced thirty different ad ideas for our last campaign. Every time, she said the same thing, "make it better!" or "make it more interesting!" We argued* all the time.'

'What was the problem?'

'Clifton wanted to advertise Gondwanaland as a place for adventure holidays. The problem was that adventure holidays attract backpackers*. Anastasia didn't like the idea.'

'Why? I was a backpacker. I loved it. It's the best way to travel.'

'This was a question of money. A backpacker in a youth hostel* doesn't spend much money on holiday. Backpackers eat sandwiches that they make from the supermarket, whereas a family of four eats in nice restaurants. They stay in expensive hotels. Families spend money and that's the kind of business that Gondwanaland wants.'

'Thanks, that's useful advice,' you say.

▶ section 220

Chapter 11

218 Section 218

You expect the water to be cold, but it is very warm. The stinger suit is thin so you don't feel too hot. Pete gives you a snorkel* and you start swimming around the reefs. The sea is incredibly clear and you have a wonderful day. When you return to the boat, you tell everyone what a great time you had under the water.

'You see?' says Anastasia. 'Gondwanaland is paradise. We can't let people be scared by these newspaper stories of killer jellyfish. We need an advertising campaign that tells people the truth.'

After you finish your swim, they take you on a boat trip around the bay. You see tropical islands and palm trees and you feel the warm sun on your face. You have never felt happier.

219 Section 219

You and Anastasia sit down as the boat moves off into the harbour*. 'Oh, I almost forgot,' you say. 'I bought you a little present. They're some sweets.'

Anastasia takes the packet from you and opens it at once. 'That's very kind of you,' she says. 'How did you know I had a sweet tooth?' She takes one of the sweets and puts it in her mouth, then passes you the packet. You eat one too, they are delicious. You look up at Anastasia and smile, but now Anastasia looks very worried. Her face is red and she takes the sweet out of her mouth. 'Are these nuts*?' she asks.

'I don't know,' you say. 'Yes, maybe.'

'I'm allergic* to nuts!' she shouts. Her face looks fatter already. She is having an allergic reaction! 'Nikos!' she shouts. 'Turn the boat around.'

Nikos and Anastasia get off the boat and run back to the Jeep. 'Come on Pete,' shouts Nikos. 'We're going to the hospital.' He glares* at you angrily.

They drive off, leaving you alone looking at the palm trees and the beautiful clear water. 'Oh no,' you think. 'I've just poisoned our most important client.'

Go back to the start of the chapter and try again.

Chapter 11

Section 220

Do you want to speak to anyone else?

1 Yes, I want to speak to Eva Campano. ▶ section 227

2 Yes, I want to speak to John Miller. ▶ section 217

3 Yes, I want to speak to Layla Evans. ▶ section 231

4 Yes, I want to speak to Sylvia Watson. ▶ section 224

5 No, I have spoken to everyone that I want. ▶ section 221

Section 221

Two days later, you fly to Gondwanaland and check into your hotel – the
Gondwana Palace. Everyone around you is talking about the composer's
death. Many people are angry about the stories in the newspapers. There
is no doubt* that people in Gondwanaland are very, very worried.

The next morning a man behind the reception desk at the hotel gives
you a handwritten note.

> Thank you so much for coming.
> Today we're going snorkelling to experience the sea around Gondwanaland.
> Please bring your swimming costume.
> We look forward to meeting you.
> Anastasia.

Do you ...

1 wear your swimming costume under casual beach clothes? ▶ section 232

2 wear formal clothes and take your swimming costume in a bag? ▶ section 223

125

Chapter 11

222 Section 222

A jeep picks you up at your hotel. It has the colourful badge* of the Gondwanaland Tourism Board on the side. It takes you to the pier* at the end of town, where a beautiful white boat is waiting for you. On the pier, you see Anastasia, Nikos and your friend Pete Deng. Anastasia is wearing a long white beach dress and sandals. Your friend Pete is in shorts and a Hawaiian shirt. Next to them is a serious looking man in his thirties. He has a smart blue polo shirt and long trousers. He is wearing deck shoes. This must be Anastasia's assistant, Nikos.

Anastasia walks confidently towards you and shakes your hand. 'So pleased to meet you,' she says. 'We all saw the Avoca Arrow advert and we thought it was simply wonderful.'

'Wonderful,' repeats Nikos.

'Good to see you again,' says Pete.

'I'm pleased you have your swimming things,' says Anastasia. 'Today, we're going to swim in our beautiful sea.'

What do you say?

1. 'I'm looking forward to it. I'm ready to dive in the water right now!' ▶ section 225

2. 'Beautiful, but dangerous too! What about the box jellyfish?' ▶ section 226

Chapter 11

Section 223

223

A jeep picks you up at your hotel. It has the colourful badge* of the Gondwanaland Tourism Board on the side. It takes you to the pier* at the end of town, where a beautiful white boat is waiting for you. On the pier, you see Anastasia, Nikos and your friend Pete Deng. Anastasia is wearing a long white beach dress and sandals. Your friend Pete is in shorts and a Hawaiian shirt. Next to them is a serious looking man in his thirties. He has a smart blue polo shirt and long trousers. This must be Anastasia's assistant, Nikos.

Anastasia walks confidently towards you and shakes* your hand. 'So pleased to meet you,' she says. 'But, I'm sorry, they didn't tell you. We're going snorkelling today. Nikos, what is the meaning of this? I specifically asked you to leave a message for our guest about wearing swimming things.'

'I did leave a note!' complains* Nikos. 'It's that hotel again. The receptionist is useless!'

What do you say?

1	'Don't worry. I have my swimming things in my bag.'	▶ section 216
2	'It's just a mistake. I'm sure we'll enjoy our boat trip anyway.'	▶ section 228

Chapter 11

224 Section 224

Unfortunately, Sylvia is not at her desk so you can't speak to her. You see Karen in the corridor. 'Do you know where Sylvia is?' you ask.

'Yes, I just saw her leaving,' replies Karen. 'Her son Jack is in trouble at school again. She had to go to see the principal.'

225 Section 225

Anastasia smiles. 'You'll love it. The sea here is beautiful, the most beautiful on earth and I'm from Greece, so I know what a beautiful sea is like. Nikos too, although he was born here.'

'My parents were from Athens,' says Nikos.

'And don't worry about the box jellyfish,' says Pete with a smile. 'We're going to wear stinger suits. They're a special sort of wetsuit*. They protect you from all jellyfish.'

'I wasn't worried,' you say. Everyone laughs and you get ready to go on the boat. You remember the presents you bought in the hotel, but you are still not sure which present to give to Anastasia.

Do you …

1	give her the wooden necklace?	▶ section 233
2	give her the expensive sweets?	▶ section 219
3	give her the African music CD?	▶ section 229
4	decide that none of the presents are suitable?	▶ section 230

226 Section 226

Anastasia looks shocked*. 'Don't believe everything you read in the newspapers,' she says.

Nikos gives you a disapproving look. 'You're here to help us, you know.'

'Don't worry,' says Pete. 'We're wearing stinger suits. They're a special sort of wetsuit*. They protect you from all jellyfish.'

Chapter 11

'Thank goodness for that,' you say. You all go on board the boat. Nikos goes last. He watches you get on the boat and he doesn't look friendly.

Section 227

Eva is sitting in her office holding her ANZA Award. She is cleaning the trophy. When you come in the room, she quickly puts the little statue back on her desk. 'Hi,' she says. 'How are things?'

'Good and bad,' you say. 'I'm going to be the new head of the Gondwanaland Account. Tomorrow I'm going up there to meet Anastasia Dimitris. Do you know her?'

'Yes, I know Anastasia. I've worked with her a lot.'

'Do you have any advice for me about her?' you ask.

'Anastasia is very professional, very demanding, but also very imaginative,' says Eva. 'You shouldn't be afraid to present new and different ideas to her. She likes that.'

'Thanks Eva. That's useful information,' you say. 'I'll let you get back to your work.'

'Thanks,' says Eva. 'I'm very busy today.'

Section 228

'Well, you can borrow a swimming costume,' says Anastasia. 'We have some on the boat, but we're definitely going to complain* to that hotel.'

You don't know what to say. The boat goes out into the open sea and you enjoy diving in the clear waters around Gondwanaland. However, after you return to your hotel you don't hear any more from Anastasia or Nikos.

The next morning, you are woken up by your mobile ringing. It is Pete Deng. 'What's going on?' he asks.

'Er, sorry?' you say. 'I don't know what you're talking about.'

'Nikos is furious* with you. He's saying you're a liar*.'

'Me?'

'Yes! Nikos phoned the hotel to complain because you didn't get his message. However, the hotel manager said he gave you the message personally. Nikos was really embarrassed*. We are the Gondwanaland Tourism Board so we need to have a good relationship with all the hotels around here.'

129

Chapter 11

'Oh no,' you say.

'It's bad news for you,' says Pete, sighing. 'Anastasia told me this morning that she's going to start working with the other ad agency because she can't trust you.'

'Can you help me, Pete?'

'No, I can't! Anastasia's cancelling the Clifton contract.'

You have lost your company's biggest contract! Without the Gondwanaland contract, Clifton will go out of business.

Go back to the start of the chapter and try again.

Section 229

⭐ You win 1 bonus point. Mark the scorecard on page 186.

You and Anastasia sit down as the boat moves off into the harbour*. 'Oh, I almost forgot,' you say. 'I bought you a little present. It's a CD by a band called *Manika 13*, from Mali.'

Anastasia takes the CD from you and pushes her glasses up on her hair. She looks at it carefully. 'That's very kind of you,' she says. 'I don't know this band, but I love African music. Thank you ever so much. My father was a musician. He used to play the guitar. He was so talented.'

As you continue into the ocean, Anastasia tells you more about her life. You have established a great relationship with your new client!

Section 230

The boat goes out into the open water. The sea is very clear, like glass. You can see brightly coloured fish under the water. There is no wind today so the sea is very calm. In the distance, you can see the beach around Gondwana Town. It shines white in the sun. 'What do you think?' asks Anastasia.

'I think it's beautiful,' you say. 'In our business, it's very important to see the product you're advertising. Being here is a great opportunity to get ideas for our ads.' You look over the side of the boat.

Pete sees your face and he laughs. 'Are you looking for box jellyfish?'

'Yes, I am,' you say. 'But I'm not worried. How do these stinger suits work?'

'Nikos, you explain,' says Anastasia.

'With pleasure,' says Nikos. 'The jellyfish can't touch your skin through a stinger suit,' he explains. 'If you wear one in the water, you'll be

Chapter 11

completely safe. Of course, you're completely safe here anyway. We don't have any box jellyfish in our waters normally. The composer, Ambrosius Smith was very unlucky.'

You put on your stinger suit. It covers your body except for your head and feet. Anastasia and Pete also put on stinger suits, but Nikos stays on the boat.

'Are you ready?' asks Anastasia.

'Are there any sharks around here?' you ask.

'Hundreds!' says Pete with a laugh, before he jumps in the water. Anastasia goes next. Finally, it is your turn. You dive into the sea.

 section 218

Section 231

When you get to her office, Layla is reading a book of poems and eating an apple.

'Shouldn't you be working?' you ask.

'I am working,' she says. 'I'm a copywriter*. I work with words. Reading poetry is a great way to get ideas.'

'I'm here for ideas too,' you say.

Layla puts her book down, but she keeps eating her apple. Through the window, you notice that the rain has stopped and the sun has come out again. 'Ideas about what?' she asks.

'I'm going to Gondwanaland to speak to Anastasia Dimitris,' you say. 'Do you have any advice about working with her?'

'Listen,' says Layla.

'I am listening,' you say.

'No,' says Layla, 'I mean listen carefully to Anastasia. She usually tells people exactly what she wants. She also understands the tourism industry very well.'

'OK,' you say.

'I wouldn't want to be Nikos though.'

'Who's Nikos?'

'He's her PA*, her personal assistant. He does everything for her. They're always together. You'll see. You're not just dealing with Anastasia,' says Layla, 'you're dealing with Nikos too.'

'Thanks Layla,' you say.

▶ section 220

131

Chapter 11

232   Section 232

You go back to your room and put your swimming costume on, then go back down to the reception area. While you are waiting, you decide it would be a good idea to buy Anastasia a small present. You go into the hotel gift* shop and see if there is anything she might like. It is very important to impress Anastasia, but it is very difficult to choose something without knowing her. The shop is very small, but in the end you find three things she might like – a brightly-coloured wooden necklace*, some expensive sweets and a music CD by a band from Mali.

233   Section 233

You and Anastasia sit down at the back of the boat. 'Oh, I almost forgot,' you say. 'I bought you a little present. It's a wooden necklace.'

Anastasia takes the necklace. 'That's very kind of you,' she says. She looks at it for a second and then puts it in her pocket. Then she says, 'OK, let's go Nikos.'

Nikos starts the boat's engine and you move slowly into the harbour*.

234   Section 234

Sylvia is just about to leave the office. She has put on her coat.

'Is something wrong?' you ask.

'It's Jack, my son. He's in trouble at school and now I have to see the school principal. Never have children! That's my advice!' she says. 'What did you want?'

'I just wanted to ask you a question,' you say. 'I'm working on the Gondwanaland account and I'm going to meet Anastasia Dimitris. What's she like?'

'She's very professional, a very high-powered manager,' says Sylvia. 'Oh, I remember one thing. She loves African music and she always complains* that she never hears about new albums up in Gondwanaland. Buy her a CD or something. She'll be your friend for life. OK?'

'OK, thanks Sylvia.'

'Sorry, I have to go now. See you later!'

This is useful information.

132

Chapter 12

Section 235

You have had a fantastic day on the yacht with Anastasia and Pete, and now you really understand the situation in Gondwanaland. Pete has accompanied you back to the door of your hotel. 'Have a good trip back to Sydney,' he says. 'I'm sure you'll come up with some great ideas for our advertising campaign* now.'

'Thanks, Pete,' you say. 'We'll be in touch soon with our ideas.'

Then Pete says something to you very quietly. 'Hey, do you see that woman in reception?'

You look at the sofas in the reception area, where you see a woman working on a laptop*. 'Yes,' you say, 'but I don't know her.'

'Her name is Kylie McQuarrie. She's an account director for the Young, McQuarrie and Street Agency. She's your competitor* for the Gondwanaland contract. She doesn't know you're here and you never saw her, right?'

'Right, Pete. Thanks for the tip.'

'OK, goodnight! Let's have a chat online soon.' Pete leaves the hotel. You are on your own.

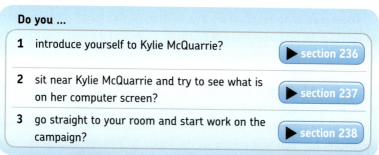

Do you ...

1. introduce yourself to Kylie McQuarrie? ▶ section 236
2. sit near Kylie McQuarrie and try to see what is on her computer screen? ▶ section 237
3. go straight to your room and start work on the campaign? ▶ section 238

Section 236

You walk into reception and stand next to Kylie McQuarrie. 'May I join you?' you ask.

'Of course,' says Kylie. She is friendly but slightly suspicious. 'Have we met before?' she asks.

Chapter 12

'I don't think so,' you say. You tell Kylie your name. 'I work for Clifton Creative Agency.'

Quickly, Kylie closes her laptop. It snaps shut. 'Oh, the competition,' she says. 'How did you recognise* me?'

'We work in the same industry,' you say. 'I guess I must recognise you from a conference or something.'

You chat about the Avoca campaign then Kylie says, 'Will you excuse me? I need to go to my room to make an important call.'

You say goodbye. You don't think any more of Kylie until you arrive back at work at Clifton in Sydney. Pete Deng is on the phone and he is very angry.

section 239

237 Section 237

You take your key card from the receptionist and walk slowly over to the sofas where Kylie McQuarrie is sitting. There are some newspapers on a coffee table so you pick one up and you pretend* to read it. You sit near to Kylie, slightly behind her. On her computer screen, there is a PowerPoint slideshow with her plans for an advertising campaign* for Gondwanaland. You sit and watch it and you see all of your competitor's* plans.

You feel a little guilty, but this is very valuable information. It is Kylie's mistake* because she is looking at confidential company information in a public place where anyone can read it, including you!

Their plan is to emphasise* the wildlife in the Gondwanaland area rather than the activities you can do there. As well as the box jellyfish, they will say it is a great area to see beautiful birds, crocodiles, tropical fish and sharks. It is a good idea. People are afraid to come to Gondwanaland because of the dangerous wildlife. This campaign turns the idea on its head. It encourages people to come and see those animals.

It will be difficult to beat the Young, McQuarrie and Street Agency campaign, but you will return to the office in Sydney with some very useful information.

section 240

238 Section 238

You quickly go into the lift. Before the doors close, you check to see if Kylie saw you. She doesn't notice you at all because she is working hard on her

Chapter 12

laptop*. No one from the Young, McQuarrie and Street Agency knows that you are in Gondwanaland.

You have lots of new ideas for the Gondwanaland campaign and you are excited to start the project. With all the stories about Ambrosius Smith's death in the media, it is very important to react fast and because you went back to your hotel room early, you can start writing the brief* for the creative team.

 section 241

Section 239

'Kylie told Anastasia that you met her,' says Pete. 'Anastasia guessed* that I told you about Kylie!'

'Sorry, Pete,' you say.

'Sorry? I could lose my job for revealing confidential company information!'

'Oh, no! I'm so sorry.'

'Yeah? Well you should be. Anastasia is furious and she's giving the new contract* to the Young, McQuarrie and Street Agency.'

You have lost your company's biggest client*! Without the Gondwanaland contract, Clifton will go out of business.

Go back to the start of the chapter and try again. section 235

Section 240

When you get back to Sydney, your first job is to write the creative brief*. Next you need to make an important decision about where to advertise. You can either advertise 'above the line' or 'below the line'. 'Above the line' is traditional advertising, using posters, ads in newspapers and magazines, or on the TV and the radio. 'Below the line' means advertising using digital media such as Facebook, Twitter and paid online adverts.

You hire a media agency to help make this decision. The agency analyses your target* customers and gives you lots of information. In this case, they advise you to advertise 'below the line'.

The creative team are happy about this. They love making digital ads because they can be much more creative than with traditional TV or

Chapter 12

poster ads. The media agency suggests a static online ad, as well as a short movie that might 'go viral'.

'Going viral' is every advertiser's dream. Instead of paying for an advert to go on websites, you rely on people enjoying it so much that they forward it to their friends, who will forward it to their friends, and so on. Very quickly an online video can be seen by hundreds of thousands of viewers and it is completely free!

241 Section 241

The creative team read your brief and the following day you speak to them about their initial ideas.

'Wildlife*,' says Eva. 'Let's focus on wildlife. They have a "problem" with jellyfish, right?'

'Yes,' you say.

'Well, the jellyfish aren't a "problem". No, the jellyfish are wildlife, and wildlife is ...'

'Wildlife is wild and exciting and dangerous,' shouts Layla, very enthusiastically. 'And something that you want to come and see!'

'Right. So instead of a problem we have an opportunity,' you say. 'I'm impressed! I mean, we can't ignore* the jellyfish!'

'I'm so glad you agree,' says Eva. 'Let's meet again at the same time tomorrow. We'll have some actual ideas to show Anastasia.'

At the next meeting, Eva presents you with two ideas. 'First, the full wildlife ad. We see people diving with sharks in cages.'

'Sharks in cages aren't very wild or dangerous!' you laugh.

'The sharks aren't in cages!' laughs Layla. 'It's the people who are in a cage – so that the sharks can't hurt them. They do it in South Africa, it's a massive* tourism hit.'

'Next, we have people snorkelling in the sea where there are jellyfish – we can actually see the jellyfish – but they're fine because they're wearing stinger suits,' says Eva. 'They're looking at the tropical fish. Then we end with a sunset scene with water birds standing at the edge of the sea with their long legs. It'll be beautiful. So, do you like it?'

'Yes. What else have you got?'

'The second idea is the same as the first, but there are no jellyfish.'

'No jellyfish?'

Chapter 12

'No jellyfish. We thought that the Gondwanaland Tourism board might not want to actually show the jellyfish. So we have the shark-diving, the snorkelling with beautiful fish, but no jellyfish, and the sunset scene.'

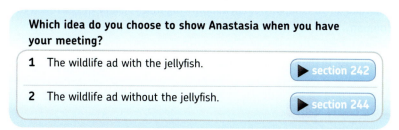

Section 242

242

Three days later, you, Karen Booth and Eva Campano fly to Gondwana Town to show Anastasia Dimitris your ideas. Karen is there because the Gondwanaland Tourism Board is such an important client, and she has known Anastasia for a long time. As you get near the meeting room, you hear Anastasia saying, 'If I hear the word "jellyfish" once more, I will scream!' She stops talking and smiles as you walk in.

Karen introduces Anastasia to the creative team and Eva starts to prepare things for her presentation. You whisper, 'No jellyfish!' but Eva doesn't hear you. You throw a pen under the table to try and get her attention.

Karen says, 'Ouch!' and looks angrily at you.

It is too late. Eva has started speaking, 'Gondwanaland hasn't got a "problem" with jellyfish. The jellyfish are just wildlife, and wildlife is exciting and dangerous and attractive. We can't ignore them–'

'Yes, we can!' says Anastasia. 'I hired you* to make the jellyfish go away, but you want to celebrate them? You must be joking! I want creative and original thinking – I do not want jellyfish. Karen, I'm sorry, I don't think Clifton understands Gondwanaland any more. It's time for us to go our separate ways.'

Anastasia picks up her handbag and marches out of the room. Nikos follows her to the door and holds it open for you. Karen looks at you and Eva, and shakes her head. You go outside to the car park and walk around, thinking for a minute. You can't believe Anastasia's reaction. Then you notice Nikos, he is talking to a woman in a car parked opposite the offices. You recognise her*, it is Kylie from the Young, McQuarrie and Street Agency.

137

Chapter 12

You travel back to Sydney in silence. Karen tells you and Eva to work from home the following day. It is nice to have a rest after the stress of the bad experience in Gondwanaland. You check your email after lunch and read an all-company email announcing that you and Eva have left the company.

Go back to the start of the chapter and try again.

243 Section 243

You organise a team meeting so that everyone can contribute ideas to the campaign*.

'OK, so we're going to run two campaigns, both of them digital. There'll be an ad that we can place on websites – it could be just an image or it could be interactive, you know, like a game or something. And we're going to make a very short film – ideally we want it to go viral. In other words, we want people to watch the film and like it so much that they share* it with friends online,' you explain. 'Normally, we'd ask the creative team to come up with all of the campaign ideas, but this is a very important project. I want everyone in the team to contribute all of their ideas before the creatives develop the best ones into detailed ad proposals.

'The idea of this meeting is to brainstorm*. Sylvia's going to write all of the ideas up on the board under two headings – online ad and film. Any idea is acceptable, so don't be shy. We'll write every idea on the board and see what we can come up with. Remember, we're focusing on the jellyfish – how can we hide this problem, or use it to our advantage? Right, who wants to start?'

'Jellyfish game,' says John.

'A jellyfish game? Can you say any more?'

'A game where you have to avoid* jellyfish that are flying towards you. You get points for avoiding them. Or it could be something like *Angry Birds*, but with jellyfish.'

'OK,' you say. 'Sylvia, let's call this idea Angry Jellyfish.'

Sylvia writes 'Angry Jellyfish' on the board and you continue, 'We can talk about Angry Jellyfish in more detail later. Let's think of some other ideas first.'

Chapter 12

'What about the ad that the Queensland Tourism Board made a few years ago?' suggests Layla. 'They made an ad for "The best job in the world". The pay was really high, like $100,000 for one year, and all you had to do was live on a beautiful tropical island for a year. The ad went viral and it was reported all around the world because it was such an amazing offer. They had hundreds of thousands of applicants[*]. It was successful because millions of people forwarded the ad to their friends, and it was all over social media and news channels. People in the street were talking about it, and all the time they were looking at the picture of this perfect tropical island in Queensland and thinking about what a great job it would be for them.'

'OK. Job ad, Sylvia.' Sylvia writes 'Job ad' on the board in the online ad category.

Section 244

244

Three days later, you, Karen Booth and Eva Campano fly to Gondwana Town to show Anastasia Dimitris your ideas. Karen is there because the Gondwanaland Tourism Board is such an important client, and she has known Anastasia for a long time. As you get near the meeting room, you hear Anastasia talking to Nikos, 'Gondwanaland's future is adventure tourism – forget the wildlife.'

Nikos nods his head and repeats what Anastasia said, 'Forget the wildlife.' They both stop talking and look up as you walk in.

Eva stands to give her presentation. 'Gondwanaland isn't so much about adventure tourism, it's really the wildlife that's exciting. We want to create an ad that gets away from the usual adventure activities. We want to focus on the animals – not the jellyfish of course, but the sharks and the fish. We want to create a short film with people diving with sharks, and snorkelling in the sea …'

'Stop!' says Anastasia firmly, with her right hand in a 'stop' sign.

Nikos echoes, 'Stop.'

'I hired you to make Gondwanaland look unique and special. This ad makes us look the same as anywhere else that has sharks and tropical fish. This isn't what I'm looking for. It's boring. I want creative and original thinking – not this! Karen, I'm sorry, I don't think Clifton understands Gondwanaland any more. It's time for us to go our separate ways.'

139

Chapter 12

Anastasia picks up her handbag and marches out of the room. Nikos follows her to the door and holds it open for you. Karen looks at you and Eva, and shakes her head. You go outside to the car park and walk around, thinking for a minute. You can't believe Anastasia's reaction. Then you notice Nikos, he is talking to a woman in a car parked opposite the offices. You recognise* her, it is Kylie from the Young, McQuarrie and Street Agency.

You travel back to Sydney in silence. Karen tells you and Eva to work from home the following day. It is nice to have a rest after the stress of the bad experience in Gondwanaland. You check your email after lunch and read an all-company email announcing that you and Eva have left the company.

Go back to the start of the chapter and try again.

245 Section 245

There are lots of ideas for the online ad, but no one has any ideas for a film. Sylvia has to go home at 5.30 p.m. to make her son's dinner, but the rest of the team stay at work. By 9.30 p.m. there are five suggestions for a film. However, you can't use any of them because they are based on Gondwanaland's wildlife* and you know that the Young, McQuarrie and Street Agency are using this idea. To win the contract* you have to do something different, something better.

You order some takeaway pizzas and coffees and the meeting continues into the night. Suddenly Eva says, 'Yes! I have it! Let's do an

Chapter 12

"anti-ad" – a film where we make the other resorts in Australia seem even more dangerous than Gondwanaland and its jellyfish! It could be like a horror film, like *Jaws* or something, with sharks attacking people on famous beaches in Sydney and Melbourne. We make those places look really scary*, then Gondwanaland will look OK because there aren't any sharks there.'

'Brilliant!' you say, and you write 'Shark attack' on the board under the film category. This seems to break the ice, and suddenly there are a lot of film suggestions. Most of them focus on action and adventure ideas. At 11.15 p.m. you end the meeting with a review of the ideas. There are about 30 online ad ideas and 9 ideas for the film.

'Eva,' you say, 'you and the creative team have one day to develop the two best ideas for each medium, that's two online ad ideas and two film ideas, OK?'

 section 246

Section 246

You have a day off and when you get back to the office you are ready to hear the creative team's proposals. You are chatting to Eva and Layla when Sylvia arrives a few minutes late. She says, 'I'm terribly sorry to be late. I have a problem today. Jack's school is closed and I haven't got anyone to look after him. Would you mind if he comes into Clifton today? I promise he'll be quiet and he won't be any trouble. He could sit there in the corner.'

What do you say?

1. 'No, I'm sorry, but this is a serious workplace. We can't have a teenager here.' section 247

2. 'Well, it isn't ideal, but if it's just for a day I suppose we can do that.' section 248

Section 247

'Oh,' says Sylvia. 'Well, in that case I need to take the day off. Is that OK?'

You want Sylvia to take the minutes* in the meeting, but you don't want Jack there too, so you say, 'Can you ask John Miller if he's free?' John is free, so he comes and takes notes while you chair* the meeting. Sylvia goes home.

Chapter 12

Eva presents two ideas to you. The first is the film idea. 'We really want to go with the shark attack film. So, the opening scene shows Sydney Harbour Bridge. Then we show a peaceful scene at Bondi Beach with all the surfers sitting on their boards waiting to catch a wave. All of a sudden, there's a huge shark which attacks the surfers. The blood turns the sea red. Then we get a message on the screen, like a football score, "People: 0 – Sharks: 7".'

'I love it!' you say.

'Next, the same in Western Australia, on a beach around Perth. One minute there are people having fun in the water, the next, there's a massive* shark attack and the message says, "People: 0 – Sharks: 9", and so on in other places like the Gold Coast and Melbourne. The film ends with a quiet beach in Gondwanaland, with families swimming and playing in the water, and the message, "People: 10 – Sharks: 0"!'

You are very happy as you are sure Anastasia will love it. You spend an hour discussing lots of ideas connected with the film. Then you hear Eva's ideas for the Angry Jellyfish game, which also sounds brilliant. You are very excited.

'Eva, you and I are flying to Gondwana Town tomorrow. Sylvia isn't here so I'll make all the arrangements. You and the creative team have the rest of the day to storyboard the film. John, can you talk to the developers about how much the game would cost? Well done team – let's go!'

Section 248

'Thanks so much, I really appreciate* it. Jack's outside in my car. I'll get him and be right back, OK?' That was a good decision. Sylvia is a great member of staff*, and although school kids can be annoying*, they do have their uses.

Eva starts her presentation. 'OK, there's good news and bad news. The bad news first. We can't make the shark film.'

'Why not?'

'John told me about it, actually,' says Layla. 'It's a legal issue. The Gondwanaland Tourism Board is a member of Tourism Australia and they can't make ads that criticise other areas in Australia.'

'Oh, no. What's the good news?'

Chapter 12

'The Angry Jellyfish game is going to work really well. I've spoken to some software developers and they already have a platform that we can use. It means we could have a demo game to look at very soon.'

'Great, we need that demo game to show Anastasia,' you say. 'And what film ideas have you got?'

'We have an idea of this couple who try to do all these things like surfing and horse-riding and they have a great time. It could be like that classic Australian movie, *Crocodile Dundee*. So we'd have a tough Aussie male and a glamorous American actress. It could be really funny.'

'It doesn't sound very exciting,' you say, 'or original. How are we supposed to sell that to Anastasia?'

'It needs more work,' agrees Eva.

Jack is sitting at the other end of the meeting room. There is music coming from his headphones. Sylvia taps her finger on the table and makes a sign with her hand, and he turns the music down.

Section 249

You and Eva arrive at Gondwana Town airport the following day at midday. You take a taxi to Gondwanaland Tourism and go straight to Anastasia's office. Nikos and Anastasia smile as you come in. 'I'm very excited!' you say. 'I can't wait to show you these ideas.'

Nikos's phone rings. 'Kylie?' he whispers. 'Now's not a good time. Call me back in fifteen minutes.'

Eva starts, 'We want to get away from the jellyfish. We want to focus on the real dangers in Australian waters. Very few people die from jellyfish stings, but what's the biggest killer in the ocean?'

Anastasia looks a bit annoyed*. 'Is that a question?' she asks.

'Yes,' you say. 'What is the most dangerous thing in the oceans around Australia?'

'Kids,' says Nikos. 'You know, in boats and that kind of thing.'

'Um, big waves?' Anastasia suggests.

'Good idea,' says Eva. 'The answer is … sharks!' She presents the shark film idea. Nikos's phone rings again and he looks serious. 'Hello again. Yes, it's fine now. I'll just leave the room,' he says. 'Please excuse me.'

Eva finishes and looks at Anastasia. 'Is that it?' asks Anastasia.

'Yes! Do you like it?'

Chapter 12

'I think it's quite funny, but we can't use it. The Gondwanaland Tourism Board is a member of Tourism Australia. There are rules about membership, and one of them is you can't make ads that criticise other areas. This film idea made me laugh, but there's no way we could use it. Listen, I think we should call it a day. I have to speak to another agency about an idea.'

In the corridor you see Nikos. He is smiling and says, 'Gondwanaland: 1 – Clifton: 0. Sorry, guys!' and then he starts to laugh. He opens the main door for you. Outside you can see Kylie from the Young, McQuarrie and Street Agency getting out of a taxi.

You didn't do your research* and you lost Clifton's biggest client.*

Go back to the start of the chapter and try again.

250 Section 250

'The other idea is much better,' continues Eva, 'It's a comedy scene with a huge* jellyfish fight on the beach.'

'Do you mean the jellyfish are fighting each other?'

'No, people are throwing jellyfish at each other. It's like a game with lots of people doing it. The beach is covered with all these giant jellyfish. Like this!' And Eva throws a giant jellyfish at you.

You scream and hit the jellyfish with your hand. It doesn't hurt – in fact, it feels like rubber. It lands on Sylvia's lap. Sylvia screams. Then Eva says, 'Ha, ha! It's just a pretend jellyfish.'

'Very funny,' you say.

'It was made for us by a company called Technix. They make models for lots of films and TV programmes.' You smile. 'I'm glad you like it,' says Eva. 'So, as I was saying, the people are throwing–'

Just at that moment, Jack starts to laugh. 'Jack!' you say, tapping the table again. Jack sits up in his chair, and pulls the earphone cable out of his phone. The room is filled with a loud pop song.

'I am so sorry.' Sylvia says.

You can see what Jack is laughing at on the screen of his phone, and then you have an idea. You hold up his phone so everyone can see the screen, and say, 'I have an idea – *Gangnam Style*.'

Chapter 12

Section 251

You are holding up Jack's phone and on the screen you can see the singer Psy who had a big hit* with *Gangnam Style* a few years ago. 'OK, I have a question. 'How did this song get millions of YouTube hits around the world? Remember, it's a song by a 35-year-old Korean singer that nobody had ever heard of before. How did he do it?'

'It went viral,' Eva says.

'Exactly. But why?'

'It was a good song,' says Layla.

'There are thousands of good songs,' you say. 'Why this one?'

'The video's funny,' says John. 'It's got a funny dance.'

'Exactly!' you say. 'People loved to copy the dance. That was why it went viral. Thousands of people started to sing the song and dance *Gangnam Style* all around the world. I mean, 15,000 people gathered in Rome for a flashmob to dance *Gangnam Style*.'

'Flashmob?' asks Sylvia.

'Oh, mum!' says Jack.

'A flashmob is when lots of people arrange to meet in a certain place at a certain time to do something together,' you explain.

'How?' asks Sylvia.

'Social media – Twitter, and so on,' you say. 'In Paris, 20,000 people joined a *Gangnam Style* flashmob. Even presidents have danced the *Gangnam Style*. And it all started with social media. People liked it, shared* it and in no time the whole world was dancing to this crazy Korean song. The point is this – if we can get a good song and people doing something that others want to copy, then we could have something very special on our hands!' We could have our own Gondwana Style dance!'

Section 252

It was lucky that you let Jack stay at Clifton. Without him, you wouldn't have had the Gondwana Style idea. You and the creative team are very excited. You need to plan quickly. The creatives spend just half a day thinking about the ad. Then you meet Eva to hear her team's ideas.

Chapter 12

'We want to have a character that dances a special dance – the Gondwana Style – with some cool* music. We will film in three different areas where you can have fun in Gondwanaland – the sea, the land and the air. We would start with sea, which is what Gondwanaland is famous for. The character dances on a surfboard or in a water-ball.'

'A water-ball?' you ask.

'Like this,' she says, and she shows you a picture of a water-ball.

'Then on land, we could have the character dancing on a mountain bike or it could be on a motocross bike – you know, a motorbike that can go off-road. The last part of the film is in the air. We were thinking of either doing something with a flying fox or bungee jumping.'

'Sorry, Eva. What's a flying fox?'

'A wire that goes from the top of one tall tree to another tree. You hold onto a handle and slide down the wire – it's really good fun! It's a great way of seeing the birds and animals that live right at the top of the jungle, and you can move quickly between trees and see different things.

'So you have some decisions to make. Which do you prefer? Let's start with the sea.'

253   Section 253

'I think we should use surfing. It's a famous Australian sport, so it will be more attractive to foreign viewers. The water-ball looks like something children might enjoy for half an hour. I mean, it isn't something you would do a lot, is it?'

'I completely agree,' says Eva. 'I didn't like the water-ball that much. Let's go with surfing. The next part of the film is on land. Shall we use

Chapter 12

mountain bikes or motocross bikes? Motocross bikes are those big, powerful motorbikes they use for going off-road. They're quite noisy!'

Section 254

'I think we should use mountain bikes. They're much cleaner than motocross.'

John and Sylvia walk in. 'How's the Gondwanaland campaign*?' John asks.

'Great, thanks,' you say. 'We're planning the film.'

'We've got surfing,' says Layla, 'and we've got mountain bikes!'

'Good choice,' says John. 'Mountain bikes are great for appreciating nature. You can stop and look at things easily.'

'OK,' says Eva. 'So we have surfing, we have mountain bikes. And the last part of the film is about the air activities. The choices are bungee-jumping or the flying fox.'

Section 255

'I think we should use the motocross bikes. They're more exciting than mountain bikes.'

'OK,' says Eva.

John and Sylvia walk in. 'How's the Gondwanaland campaign*?' John asks.

'Great, thanks,' you say. 'We're planning the film.'

'We've got surfing,' says Layla, 'and we've got motocross!'

Chapter 12

'But you can't use a motocross bike for the film!' says Sylvia. 'Not for Anastasia. Her husband, Leo, had a terrible accident a few years ago. He was in hospital for months.'

'Right! No motocross bikes.' you say. 'Thanks, Sylvia, what would we do without you?'

'OK,' says Eva. 'So we have surfing, we have mountain bikes. And the last part of the film is about the air activities. The choices are bungee-jumping or the flying fox.'

What do you choose?

1. bungee-jumping ▶ section 257
2. flying fox ▶ section 258

256 Section 256

'I think we should use the water-ball. It's different and unusual. And the character would look funny dancing in a huge* plastic ball.'

Layla runs in. 'I've just done some research into water-balls. They can't use them in Gondwanaland because of the coral.'

'What?'

'There are a lot of rocks under the water in Gondwanaland. If a water-ball touched a sharp rock, it would rip and the ball would collapse. It could be dangerous!'

'Oh! Then we should use surfing in the film!' you say. 'Well done, Layla. That saved us from some future problems.'

'Great,' says Eva. 'The next part of the film is on land. Shall we use mountain bikes or motocross bikes?'

'Motocross bikes?'

'They're those big, powerful motorbikes they use for going off-road. They're really fast!'

What do you choose?

1. motocross bikes ▶ section 255
2. mountain bikes ▶ section 254

Chapter 12

Section 257

'OK!' says Eva. 'So, to sum up, we have surfing, mountain biking and bungee-jumping. Next, we need to decide what kind of character to use. We think that either a koala or a crocodile would be a good animal to represent Gondwanaland. We can use a cartoon animation of the animal and it would be added to the film afterwards, so it looks like it's doing all these activities.'

'We're thinking of "Krazy Koala" or "Krazy Croc" as names for the characters,' adds Layla. 'What do you think?'

You say, 'To be honest, I like them both. A koala and a crocodile are both really good animals to use. Let's keep both Krazy Koala and Krazy Croc for the moment. OK, folks – now for the big moment. I'm going to tell Karen about the plans. This is a very important campaign and we have to make sure we get everything right. We can't afford to lose the Gondwanaland contract*, so ... wish me luck!'

Section 258

'OK!' says Eva. 'So to sum up, we have, surfing, mountain biking and the flying fox. Next, we need to decide what kind of character to use. We think that either a koala or a crocodile would be a good animal to represent Gondwanaland. We can use a cartoon animation of the animal and it would be added to the film afterwards, so it looks like it's doing all these activities.

'We're thinking of "Krazy Koala" or "Krazy Croc" as names for the characters,' adds Layla. 'What do you think?'

You say, 'To be honest, I like them both. A koala and a crocodile are both really good animals to use. Let's keep both Krazy Koala and Krazy Croc for the moment. OK, folks – now for the big moment. I'm going to tell Karen about the plans. This is a very important campaign and we have to make sure we get everything right. We can't afford to lose the Gondwanaland contract*, so ... wish me luck!'

Chapter 12

259 Section 259

You are in Karen's office. 'I like Krazy Koala and Krazy Croc, they're both nice and it's good to give Anastasia some choices,' she says.

'Thanks,' you say. 'So, in the film we want to show the three different aspects of Gondwanaland: the sea, the land and the air. The slogan* is "Gondwanaland – there's more to see than sea".'

'That's good,' Karen says.

'Our animal character is going to dance on a surfboard in the ocean, dance on land while he's mountain biking and dance in the air – bungee-jumping.'

'Bungee-jumping? Are you mad? Bungee jumping has made New Zealand a world-famous adventure-sports destination. We can't associate Gondwanaland with bungee-jumping!'

'Oh, of course. The other idea we had was a flying fox.'

'That sounds much better.'

That evening at home, you are relaxing on your balcony. 'What a week!' you think. You are about to go to Gondwanaland to make the most important presentation of your career – or rather, Eva Campano is going to make the most important presentation of your career. You are glad* you don't have to pitch* the idea yourself – that would be really stressful.

You are happy with the last-minute preparations. A popular Australian singer has composed a great song for the film and you have hired a brilliant choreographer to plan the dance moves to go with the music. Everything is going according to plan. What could go wrong now?

 section 261

260 Section 260

⭐ You win 1 bonus point. Mark the scorecard on page 186.

You are in Karen's office. 'In the film we want to show the three different aspects of Gondwanaland: the sea, the land and the air. The character in the film is going to have a special dance, like *Gangnam Style*. He's going to dance on a surfboard in the ocean, dance on land while he's mountain biking and dance in the air while he's on a flying fox. We think people will want to copy the dance and the Gondwana Style could become a viral hit.'

150

Chapter 12

Karen looks very happy. You explain about the koala and the crocodile, you talk about the popular Australian singer who is composing the music and about the brilliant choreographer who is planning the dance moves to go with the music. Then you tell her the slogan*, 'Gondwanaland – there's more to see than sea.'

'I love it!' laughs Karen. 'And I really like Krazy Koala and Krazy Croc, too. They're really nice and it's good to give Anastasia some choices. Remember that she may be sensitive about the crocodile being another "dangerous animal". She's very upset about the whole jellyfish thing. On the other hand, the koala may be too soft. Judge her mood on the day and make the decision then. I trust you on this.'

'Thanks,' you say.

That evening at home, you are relaxing on your balcony. 'What a week!' you think. You are about to go to Gondwanaland to make the most important presentation of your career – or rather, Eva Campano is going to make the most important presentation of your career. You are glad* you don't have to pitch* the idea yourself – that would be really stressful. Everything is going according to plan. What could go wrong now?

Chapter 13

261 Section 261

You and Eva fly to Gondwanaland to pitch* your ideas to Anastasia. On the morning of the meeting you are waiting for Eva outside the hotel and feeling nervous. You are glad* you are the account director. It is Eva's job, as the creative director, to actually present the ideas. You just have to smile and be friendly. Finally, Eva joins you, but she doesn't look happy.

'What's wrong?' you ask.

'I've lost my voice,' she whispers. It is almost impossible to hear her.

'But we're giving the presentation today!' you say.

'You'll have to give the presentation,' she says in a very quiet voice. 'I can't speak.'

You feel even more nervous. You are fighting for the survival of Clifton Creative Agency and even Eva can't help you now. You call a taxi and get inside. There is an advert on the radio and you hear a familiar voice.

'The Avoca Arrow. It's a tough nut* to crack!'

You remember how you managed to keep the Avoca contract and you feel a little better. When you arrive, Pete Deng is waiting outside the office and he greets you both. He takes you into reception and says, 'I think you'll find this is a good place to wait,' then he adds very quietly, 'and listen.'

The reception is next to the main meeting room. It isn't possible to see through the frosted glass, but you can hear everything. Listening carefully, you realise that your pitch is the second one of the day. The Young, McQuarrie and Street Agency have already started their presentation and you can hear Kylie McQuarrie's voice in the next room.

262 Section 262

Kylie McQuarrie is playing a video. You can hear the voice-over*. It sounds like a film trailer. 'Gondwanaland is paradise on earth,' says the voice. 'It's a land of kangaroos, crocodiles, tropical fish and beautiful birds. Dense rainforests cover its interior and no human being has ever walked on some of its remote beaches.' You imagine the video images that accompany the man speaking. The voice continues, 'The great white shark, saltwater

Chapter 13

crocodiles, silent tree snakes. This is the real planet earth, with all its beauty and excitement. Gondwanaland. Are you brave enough?'

The film ends with dramatic music. You and Eva look at each other in panic. 'That video must have cost about $20,000!' whispers Eva.

'Young, McQuarrie and Street must be desperate to win the contract from us,' you say.

Just then, the door of the meeting room opens. Nikos walks out with Kylie McQuarrie. 'Thank you so much for coming today,' he says.

'It was our pleasure,' says Kylie.

'Please excuse me a moment and I'll arrange a taxi for you,' he says to her.

You are left alone in reception with Kylie. There is an embarrassing silence while you all wait in reception. Then Kylie looks at you more carefully. She looks away and then stares* at your face again. You feel nervous. 'Excuse me,' she says. 'Have we met before?'

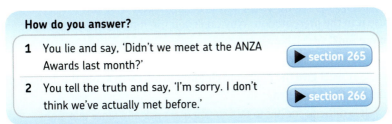

Section 263

'Our pitch is completely different from the Young, McQuarrie and Street Agency pitch,' you say.

'How do you know that?' asks Anastasia, with raised* eyebrows.

'We just heard their talk while we were waiting in reception,' you say. 'Please, Anastasia, this is a complete misunderstanding. I did sit near Kylie in that hotel, but I didn't spy on her. Why would I? I didn't know who she was back then.'

'I suppose so,' Anastasia says. 'We'll hear your presentation anyway.' She leads you into the meeting room.

You give your presentation, but there is a bad atmosphere in the room. Anastasia doesn't look happy with anything you say and Nikos doesn't seem to be listening.

Chapter 13

When you get back to Sydney, you are not surprised to learn that your pitch wasn't good enough. Karen Booth and the Clifton board are very angry that the Young, McQuarrie and Street Agency are going to handle Gondwanaland's advertising from now on.

Clifton may go bankrupt. You and Eva are sacked* immediately.

Go back to the start of the chapter and try again.

264 Section 264

'Our presentation isn't as good as theirs!' says Eva.

'What can we do?' you ask.

'I have an idea,' she says. She opens a bag and shows you a strange ball of plastic.

'What's that?' you ask.

'It's the model jellyfish,' she says. 'I brought it in case we wanted to use it in the presentation. Why don't you use it to make our presentation more fun?'

'What can I say about it?' you ask.

'Say we'll give the puppet to children to tell them about the dangers of the jellyfish,' says Eva.

It is difficult for her to talk so you don't ask any more questions.

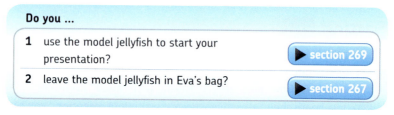

265 Section 265

'No,' says Kylie, 'I wasn't at the ANZA Awards, but your face does look familiar.' She bites her lip. You look at your watch and you wish that Nikos would come back. 'Ah! I know!' says Kylie. 'You were at the same hotel as me when I was last here at Gondwana Town. I never forget a face. I was in reception writing my presentation and you sat next to me. Wait a minute ...' She looks at your hand. You are holding a folder with the letters CCA in

Chapter 13

big gold letters next to the company logo. 'You work for Clifton!' Kylie shouts. 'You were spying on me!'

'No, not at all. I'd never do a thing like that,' you say, but Kylie is furious*. She walks very quickly into the meeting room and starts speaking in a quiet but serious voice to Anastasia. It is clear that she is very angry. Soon, Nikos arrives and leads Kylie away to a waiting taxi, giving you a very cold look over his shoulder.

Anastasia comes out of the meeting room. 'The Young, McQuarrie and Street Agency are extremely unhappy with you,' she says. 'Obviously, nobody broke the law, but perhaps it would be better if we forget about your pitch. I'll speak to Karen about it. I'm very sorry this has happened.'

'That's not fair!' you say. 'I didn't see anything on Kylie's laptop*. All our ideas are our own.'

 section 263

Section 266

Kylie smiles. You look nervously out of the window. Eva takes a sweet out of her bag for her sore throat. You all wait in an uncomfortable silence. Finally Nikos returns. 'Please come this way, Kylie,' he says. 'We'll be ready for the Clifton presentation in just a moment,' he adds looking at you.

Suddenly, Kylie realises you are her competition from Clifton. She is about to say something, but Nikos leads her out of the room.

Eva points at her bag and says, 'Come here.'

 section 264

Section 267

You go into the meeting room. There is a long wooden table in the centre. Through the windows you can see a line of palm trees. Anastasia, Nikos and Eva sit down while you prepare your laptop*. Eva can see that you are nervous. She smiles at you. When you are ready, you begin your presentation.

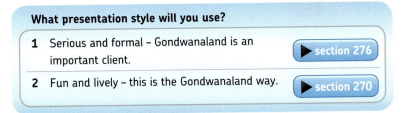

Chapter 13

268 Section 268

Nikos starts playing the part of the game that you have not seen before. Everyone is watching him play the game on the big screen. Krazy Koala is in the sea and he has a cricket bat in his hand. Everybody laughs when they see this. Then jellyfish start to fly out of the sea. Nikos isn't sure what to do. He presses buttons and the cricket bat moves. Every time the cricket bat hits a jellyfish, it explodes and you win one point.

'Horrible!' he says. 'This is horrible!'

'What were you thinking?' says Anastasia. 'This is completely inappropriate.'

'Inappropriate!' repeats Nikos.

'Part of our role is to promote respect for wildlife* and the natural environment of Gondwanaland,' says Anastasia. 'Do you think your game does that? This encourages people to kill wild animals. It's wrong in so many ways that I just don't know what to say to you.'

'If the state governor saw this,' says Nikos, 'we'd lose our jobs.'

'I think we've seen enough of the game,' says Anastasia. 'Turn it off please.' There is silence in the room. 'I'll speak to Karen next week,' says Anastasia, but you already know what she is thinking.

After a few days, the phone call comes. Anastasia explains that your proposal was rejected* and that the Gondwanaland Tourism board won't continue working with Clifton.

You have lost your company's most important customer!

Go back to the start of the chapter and try again.

269 Section 269

You go into the meeting room. There is a long wooden table in the centre. Through the windows you can see a line of palm trees. Anastasia, Nikos and Eva sit down while you connect your laptop* to the projector. When you are ready, you take Eva's advice. You reach into the bag and pull out the rubber jellyfish. 'Good morning, everyone. I want to introduce you to Boxer!'

Chapter 13

'What is that?' asks Nikos.

'It's a box jellyfish,' you say. 'For children.'

'Do you want to encourage children to play with box jellyfish?' asks Anastasia. 'They can kill!'

Eva tries to speak, but she can't so she has to stay silent.

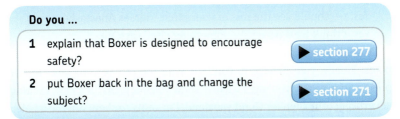

Section 270

You begin your presentation in a less formal, more conversational style. 'Hello everyone. We're very excited to show you our new ad campaign for Gondwanaland. We're sure that you're going to love it. We all know that there's a problem because of the box jellyfish. Everyone around here is really upset after the tragic death of Ambrosius Smith. The number of tourists is dropping* and many hotels are going to be empty in the busiest month of the year. People are staying away from Gondwanaland and we have to get them back. We want to change the way people think about the region. Let's stop thinking about the sea and start thinking about all the other great things you can do here.'

Anastasia smiles. You continue, 'The ad campaign that we've put together is young and clever. We are going to use new media – the internet, mobile phones, Facebook and Twitter. We want our ads to "go viral". So we'll stick* the ad online and the kids will love it. They'll send it to their friends and put it on Facebook. If we're lucky, they'll blog about it too. Basically, our end users will do our advertising for us. How can we do that? Here is our idea ...'

Chapter 13

271 Section 271

'That's obviously inappropriate,' you say. 'We were thinking outside the box.' You cough nervously. 'Outside the box – box jellyfish? Ha, ha!' Nobody laughs at your joke. Eva looks very disappointed. 'That wasn't the real point of my pitch,' you say.

'Yes, we should see the rest of your pitch,' agrees Anastasia.

'Yes, I think we'd better see something else,' says Nikos.

You are more nervous now and you can't find the right place in Eva's notes. Finally, you manage to continue with the rest of your talk. 'In our presentation today,' you say, 'I'd like to show you our plans for a new, exciting advertising campaign for Gondwanaland. I'm going to show you the ad idea and I'm also going to tell you how we're going to get everyone to see it.'

Eva nods happily. Now your presentation sounds good. You continue, 'We haven't recorded an ad yet because we want to be able to respond to your ideas. Please stop me at any time if you have any questions. OK, let's look at the first slide.'

Do you ...
1 present Krazy Croc? ▶ section 273
2 present Krazy Koala? ▶ section 278

272 Section 272

'It's nice,' says Anastasia, 'but it's missing something.'

'Yes, missing something,' says Nikos.

'Do you have something else you can show us?'

You remember the computer game. Unfortunately, you have only seen the first level of the game so you don't know if it all works. You are a bit worried about showing it to them in case there are any problems with it.

Do you ...
1 show them the game? ▶ section 281
2 say 'sorry, that's everything.'? ▶ section 283

Section 273

'Our aim is to show people that Gondwanaland is not just about the sea. There are lots of other activities that people can do too. So in our ad, we'll begin in the sea with a shot of a surfboard fin. It could be a shark's fin. Then we pan out and we see that it's an upside-down surfboard with a cartoon crocodile hanging onto it. Krazy Croc turns the board over, catches a big wave and surfs in to the beach, but he doesn't just surf – he does a crazy dance. It's fun and easy to copy.

'Then we see Krazy Croc running up the beach and jumping onto a mountain bike. He rides the bike through the jungle, while dancing the same crazy dance on the bike. Krazy Croc arrives at a huge* tree with a rope ladder. He looks up and there's a nature-viewing platform at the top. He climbs up, looks through some binoculars while doing his dance, then he jumps on a zip wire and dances through the air. When he gets to the ground, he starts dancing with lots of cool* people, doing a really fun dance that kids will want to copy.

'The slogan* is, "Gondwanaland – there's more to see than sea". This focuses attention away from the sea and the jellyfish.'

'I see,' says Anastasia. 'So you show people that we have beaches, jungles, adventure holidays and nightlife too. It's very interesting.'

'Interesting,' says Nikos as he taps some information into his tablet.

Eva smiles and gives you the thumbs up. The meeting continues for some time, until finally you shake hands and leave.

'We'll be in touch soon,' says Anastasia.

Chapter 13

274 | Section 274

⭐ You win 1 bonus point. Mark the scorecard on page 186.

Without warning, you play the music. You and Eva stand up and you start doing the dance, copying the dance moves that Krazy Koala does in the storyboard.

'You see!' you shout over the music. 'It's like *Gangnam Style*! The dance is a bit silly, but it's fun and anyone can do it. If we can get the kids doing the Gondwana Style, we could have a video that goes all around the world.'

Surprisingly, Anastasia starts to laugh. She stands up and does some of the dance with you. Her necklace* rattles as she copies the dance moves. 'I get it,' she laughs. 'It's fun. Nikos, come on!'

'I don't dance,' says Nikos and he stays in his seat. When the music stops, everyone sits down. Anastasia's hair is untidy for the first time, but she is laughing. Nikos is smiling too.

'That's great!' says Anastasia. 'My daughters would love that.'

'I can imagine my nephew and niece doing the Gondwana Style, too,' says Nikos.

Anastasia smiles. 'These are fantastic ideas!' she says. 'I can't believe that we wasted* our time with Young, McQuarrie and Street. Nikos, get Pete in here! I want to see him do the dance. He has the best moves in the office!' Nikos gets Pete Deng and they come into the meeting room together. 'Come on Pete!' says Anastasia. 'We're going to dance the Gondwana Style!'

You play the song again and everyone starts dancing the Gondwana Style, with the exception of Nikos, but even he is smiling. There is no doubt* you have won the pitch. The Gondwanaland Tourism Board loved your presentation!

275 | Section 275

Three days later, you are having coffee with John Miller in your office when suddenly Karen comes into the room. Her face is white and she is shaking. 'What did you do in Gondwanaland?' she asks.

'We just presented our plans,' you say. 'I thought the presentation went well.'

Chapter 13

'Went well?' says Karen. 'Went well? It was a disaster! They've dropped us. We've lost the Gondwanaland contract!'

John Miller drops his coffee on his desk. It spills all over his keyboard and his tie. 'Oh, no,' he says, shocked*.

'Oh, no!' you reply. 'What went wrong?'

'Anastasia said your presentation was all about dangerous animals: box jellyfish, crocodiles ...' says Karen. 'You were not supposed to talk about Gondwanaland as a dangerous place for tourists.'

'The crocodile was a cartoon, as you know,' you say. 'A joke.'

'Unfortunately, the joke's on us. You judged the mood wrongly,' says Karen. 'We've lost the contract and we're going to go out of business.'

You hold your head in your hands. All you can hear is John cleaning up the coffee from his keyboard.

Go back to the start of the chapter and try again.

Section 276

You begin your presentation in a formal style. 'Ladies and gentlemen, good morning. It gives me great pleasure to present our new ad campaign for Gondwanaland. As you are aware, this has been a difficult year for the region. The tragic death of Ambrosius Smith shocked the local community and the world. Irresponsible journalists have been writing stories about the dangers of the region. As a result, the number of visitors has fallen* and many hotel bookings have been cancelled for the holiday season. We need to find ways of repairing the damage. We have therefore been looking at ways of making people feel excited about Gondwanaland again.'

Anastasia looks impressed*. You continue, 'The advertising campaign* we have developed uses new media – the internet, mobile phones, Facebook and Twitter. Our intention is to create a campaign that will "go viral". In other words, we will create an advertisement and put it online. We believe the public will then share* or forward the advert to their friends and contacts, reaching many more end users than a traditional campaign. In effect, our target* market will do the promotion for us.

'How can this be achieved?' you ask. 'Here is the campaign that we have planned. We need to find a way of telling people about the good things in the region.'

161

Chapter 13

277 Section 277

⭐ You win 1 bonus point. Mark the scorecard on page 186.

'The idea here is that Boxer is fun,' you explain. 'Kids love to play with toys and we can give these rubber jellyfish free to families. Then people will know what the box jellyfish looks like and they'll know to avoid* them.'

'I see what you're saying,' says Anastasia, 'but we really don't want to talk about the box jellyfish. They're very rare on our beaches. The accident with Ambrosius Smith was a million-to-one chance. It will never happen again. I think your idea is very creative, but it won't work for us.'

'No, it won't work for us,' says Nikos. 'But may I ask a question here?'

'Certainly,' you say.

'Can you make other animals like this? I mean, it's a good idea and kids will love them. If we had another animal, maybe we could give them out to people.'

'We have contacts at a company that specialises in these models.'

'Really?' says Anastasia, sounding very interested. 'This could be a very clever idea to get people interested in our region. I like it!'

You are glad that you took the risk* of taking out the rubber jellyfish and that you had the confidence to carry on* and explain why educational toys can be a good marketing tool.

'I agree,' says Nikos. 'People love cartoon characters, especially animals. If only we could think of one.'

'Actually, we've already done that,' you say.

162

Chapter 13

Section 278

278

'So in our ad,' you say, 'we'll begin in the sea with a shot of a surfboard fin. It could be a shark's fin. Then we pan out and we see that it's an upside-down surfboard with a cartoon koala hanging on to it. Krazy Koala turns the board over, catches a big wave and surfs in to the beach, but he doesn't just surf – he does a crazy dance. It's fun and easy to copy.

'Then we see Krazy Koala running up the beach and jumping onto a mountain bike. He rides the bike through the jungle, while dancing the same crazy dance on the bike. He arrives at a huge* tree with a rope ladder. Krazy Koala looks up and there's a nature-viewing platform at the top. He climbs up, looks through some binoculars while doing his dance, then he jumps on a zipwire and dances through the air. When he gets to the ground, he starts dancing with lots of cool* people, doing a really fun dance that kids will want to copy.

'The slogan* is, "Gondwanaland – there's more to see than sea". This focuses attention away from the sea and the jellyfish.'

Anastasia and Nikos stare at you in silence. Nikos is wearing sunglasses and you can't see his eyes. Anastasia is holding up a drawing of the koala with both hands, like a doctor looking at an X-ray.

Before the meeting, you and Eva made an agreement. You have a secret sign that you will make if you want to start doing the Krazy Koala dance together – the Gondwana Style.

Eva gives you the sign.

163

Chapter 13

> **Do you ...**
> 1 dance the Gondwana Style with Eva? ▶ section 274
> 2 decide it is better to wait? ▶ section 272

279 Section 279

'So in our ad, we will begin in the sea with a shot of a surfboard fin. It could be a shark's fin. Then we pan out and we see that it's an upside-down surfboard with a cartoon crocodile hanging onto it. Krazy Croc turns the board over, catches a big wave and surfs in to the beach, but he doesn't just surf – he does a crazy dance. It's fun and easy to copy.

'Then we see Krazy Croc running up the beach and jumping onto a mountain bike. He rides the bike through the jungle, while dancing the same crazy dance on the bike. Krazy Croc arrives at a huge tree with a rope ladder. He looks up and there's a nature-viewing platform at the top. He climbs up, looks through some binoculars while doing his dance, then he jumps on a zip wire and dances through the air. When he gets to the ground, he starts dancing with lots of cool* people, doing a really fun dance that kids will want to copy.

'The slogan* is, "Gondwanaland – there's more to see than sea". This focuses attention away from the sea and the jellyfish.'

'I see,' says Anastasia. 'So you show people that we have beaches, jungles, adventure holidays and nightlife too. It's very interesting.'

164

Chapter 13

'Interesting,' says Nikos as he taps some information into his tablet.
'However, I don't like the idea of the crocodile,' says Anastasia.
'No crocodile, oh no,' says Nikos.

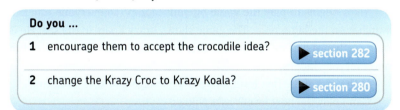

Section 280

'That's easy to fix*,' you say. 'We also thought about a koala instead of a crocodile. Eva, do you have the drawings?'

Eva gives you pictures of the other character, Krazy Koala. You show this image to Anastasia and Nikos. You play the music for the dance in your viral ad, the Gondwana Style.

'Yes, that might work,' says Anastasia. 'A koala is fun, safe and cuddly. It doesn't make you think of dangerous animals in the water, like the crocodile. I think this Krazy Koala could work.'

'Yes, Krazy Koala,' says Nikos quietly. He taps very fast on his tablet screen. When he has finished, he looks at his boss. 'May I interrupt?' he says.

'Of course,' you say.

'It's just, there's something missing. Do you have any other ideas for us? I mean something that will make the campaign seem more complete.'

You remember the computer game. Unfortunately, you have only played the first level so you don't know if it works properly. You are a bit worried about showing it to Anastasia and Nikos.

Section 281

'As well as the ad with the Krazy Koala, we also began work on a computer game for Gondwanaland,' you explain. 'It's an app which will work on a smart phone or tablet.'

'Do you have a demo?' Nikos asks.

165

Chapter 13

'Yes, we've asked our developers to produce a mini-version of the game. We have it here. You can play it. Who'd like to try?'

'You do it, Nikos,' says Anastasia.

Nikos begins to play the game on your laptop* so everyone else can watch it on the big screen. The game shows Krazy Koala in the sea. He is on a surfboard and he has to ride over some big waves. It is a lot of fun and everyone laughs.

At the end of the first level, there is a message that says 'Continue'.

'Can I play the next level?' asks Nikos.

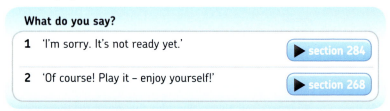

282 Section 282

'Eva and I discussed this for a long time,' you say. 'We agreed that the crocodile was the best suggestion for the ad campaign because it's more dynamic. We really think it's a winner.'

'Do you?' asks Anastasia. When she looks at you, her blue eyes seem very cold. Nikos taps* something into his tablet. The meeting ends and you feel that something isn't quite right.

Two weeks later, you have heard nothing from the Gondwanaland Tourism Board so Karen phones Anastasia. When Karen comes into your office afterwards, her face is white. You and John Miller stop working.

'What happened?' you ask.

'Gondwanaland didn't like the campaign ideas,' she says. 'They feel that we didn't understand their needs. Anastasia said that we didn't follow their instructions. We've lost the contract*.'

'Oh, no,' says John. 'Don't tell me that Young, McQuarrie and Street got it!'

'No, they didn't,' says Karen. 'Nobody got the contract. Both pitches were unsuccessful.'

'I always said that it's very difficult to please Anastasia,' says John.

Chapter 13

'It makes no difference to us,' says Karen. She pauses before she speaks again. 'That contract was essential. ANZA Award or not, now Clifton is going to go out of business.'

Go back to the start of the chapter and try again.

Section 283

283

Your presentation comes to an end. Nikos goes out to take a call. Anastasia gets up and looks at your storyboards. 'Advertising is a funny business,' she says. 'I mean, you show me campaign ideas and sometimes I personally don't like them. However, I know that my opinion is not the same as young people today. I have to trust the experts. The koala seems a bit silly to me.'

'People like silly things,' you say. 'They'll like the dance. Little kids will like it because it's fun. Teenagers and older people will like it in an ironic way. The music is great.'

'Yes,' says Anastasia. 'I think my teenage daughters would like it.'

'The important thing is to get people talking about the ad,' you say. 'At the moment, people are only talking about Gondwanaland because of the jellyfish. Let's get them to talk about something fun.'

'This is fun,' says Anastasia. 'I'll call Karen next week to let her know my final decision, but I do like this idea. It's growing on me.'

You have a good feeling about your ad, and two days later Karen comes into your office. 'I just had Anastasia on the phone,' she says.

'Already?' you say. 'Is it good news or bad news?'

'It's all good!' says Karen. 'The Gondwanaland Tourism Board have given the green light to the Gondwana Style and the Krazy Koala campaign. Clifton is in business!'

Section 284

284

'That's no problem,' says Anastasia. 'I think you've played that game enough, Nikos. We are in a meeting.'

Angrily, Nikos stops the game. 'You must remember that we don't want anything violent,' he says.

Chapter 13

'We understand that,' you say.

'Well,' says Anastasia. 'Thank you for your hard work. You have a lot of good ideas. I'll be in contact in the next week or so.'

After the meeting, you return to Sydney. As you get off the plane at the airport, you turn on your mobile phone. You have a message from Karen.

You have saved the Gondwanaland contract for Clifton! Now the hard work really begins. You need to make the ad – and make sure it goes viral.

Chapter 14

Section 285

You are on your balcony worrying about work. It is two months since you won the contract* for the new Gondwanaland campaign*. Three weeks ago, you launched* it at a big event at a luxury golf course near Gondwana Town. Since then, nothing much has happened. Visitor numbers are still very low. If you Google search 'Gondwanaland', all you see are images of jellyfish.

You look at your phone. You have a voicemail message. It is from Nikos.

'Hello. This is Nikos. I want to speak to you about the new Gondwanaland campaign. We're not happy. Not happy at all! We paid $2million for this campaign. We believed your promises. Remember? You said the film would go viral. You said it'd be a massive* success. So far, we've had just 374 views for the film. That's pathetic! My grandmother had more hits when she uploaded a video of her cat … and the cat was sleeping! The point is, this viral video is not viral! We need some results and we need them fast! Do what you have to do. That's all.'

Clifton has a PR* and marketing department, which makes sure the campaigns are promoted in the right way, but this time it hasn't worked. The media coverage of the campaign has actually made the situation worse. All the news stories are still about the jellyfish incident with Ambrosius Smith and say that the Gondwanaland Tourism Board is trying to hide the truth. None of the news channels have mentioned Krazy Koala or the Gondwana Style dance.

'Why is it so hard to deal with the media?' you ask yourself. 'How can we create media stories that are positive?' You hear a dog barking* somewhere nearby. Every time it barks it makes you jump a little. It reminds you of Dagmar. You wonder what Hans and Dagmar are doing right now.

Tomorrow morning you have a meeting with the head of marketing, Jaspal Harris. You need a new strategy and lots of new ideas. You decide to go to bed early and get a good night's sleep.

Chapter 14

286 Section 286

The next day, you feel fresh and full of energy. As you drive down the coast to Manly, you feel confident* that you can get this ad to be seen by millions of people. You start to think about all the people you could contact – it is going to be a busy day!

As you are driving past Collaroy Beach, you notice a crowd of people. They are watching an old man on the beach. He seems to be doing some kind of yoga or kung fu.

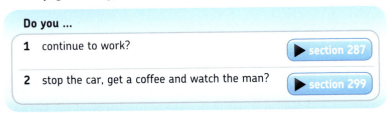

287 Section 287

The head of marketing, Jaspal Harris, meets your team at 10.00 a.m. to brainstorm* more marketing strategies for Gondwanaland. You have to get more views of the Gondwana Style video.

'We have a Facebook page that links to the YouTube video,' Jaspal says. 'I want everyone to share* this on Facebook, or just "like" the video, and share it on email and Twitter. I know we did this a few weeks ago, but we need to do it again. Sylvia, please ask all employees to email their personal contacts and friends, and ask them to watch the video and to recommend it to others.'

'I can ask Jack to help. He and his friends are good at that sort of thing,' says Sylvia.

'I have a friend who works for the Melbourne Morning Post.' says Layla. 'He's in the sports department, but maybe he can get someone to review the film for the paper.'

'The Angry Koala game is a good way to get people to click through and watch the film. Let's start talking about it on forums and add comments on blogs, maybe people can find out about it that way,' says Jaspal.

'Good ideas, team,' you say. 'Does anyone know any famous people? A celebrity* could really help us.' No one answers your question. 'I'll look at our list of media contacts for our main foreign markets – the UK, the US and

Chapter 14

China – and I'll call the biggest ones.'

You end the meeting with, 'Let's meet again tomorrow morning. We have to move quickly. I'm under a lot of pressure from the Gondwanaland Tourism Board to produce results.'

Section 288

You find the main number for Steve's Stunts and then dial Steve's personal extension.

'Hi Steve,' you say. 'How are things in Alice Springs?'

'Great,' he replies. 'We're making a movie with the next Hollywood sensation – Livia Luz. There are lots of driving scenes, so I'm really busy.'

'Livia Luz? Lucky you! She's a fantastic actress!'

'Yeah, Livia's great, and a really nice person too. Oh, by the way, congratulations on the Gondwanaland campaign.'

'Thanks,' you say. 'It's going quite well.'

'Yeah, I love that dance – the Gondwana Style. In fact, I taught it to Livia and we dance it while we're waiting for the cameras.'

'Really?' you say. 'Could you send me a video of you two dancing?'

'We'll see,' he says. 'Look, I've got to go now. Good luck!'

You forget all about the conversation with Steve, but that evening you get a text message from him with a short video clip attached. You watch it – it is him and Livia Luz doing the Gondwana Style dance! You call Steve again. 'Steve?' you say. 'Is this a good moment? It's about the video. Listen, I have to ask you a big favour*. Could you ask Livia to upload that video to her blog page?'

'I don't see why not. She's always posting photos and videos up there.'

'She has 27 million Twitter followers all around the world! If she tweeted* a link to the video, it could make a huge* difference to the campaign.'

'Leave it with me,' says Steve.

Chapter 14

289 Section 289

You give Sylvia $400 in cash*. A week later, Sylvia comes to your office. 'It's about Jack,' she says.

'Oh?' you say. 'Has he done the flashmob yet?'

'I'm sorry. I ... I don't know how to say this. Jack took the money and he spent it with his friends. I don't know, they just wasted it on parties and things like that.'

'What about our flashmob?' you ask.

'It's not going to happen,' says Sylvia. 'As he didn't do any work experience, the school said he has to repeat the year. I ... I don't know what I'm going to do with that boy. I'm sorry.' Sylvia seems very sad. She collapses in a chair and starts to cry.

'Don't worry, Sylvia, it's not your fault,' you say. 'We'll think of something else.' Unfortunately, you don't have any new ideas and the Gondwana Style ad doesn't go viral.

The Gondwanaland Tourism Board leave Clifton when the contract ends.

Go back to the start of the chapter and try again.

290 Section 290

The following day, you all meet again. Jaspal begins, 'A blog on Wordpress has mentioned the Angry Koala. It wasn't a great review, but the guy has 18,000 followers and some of them will play the game, I'm sure.'

'Good,' you say. 'I've called about 30 organisations in Europe, the States and Asia. I think some of them will write about us.'

'Not much luck with the celebrity angle, I'm afraid,' says Layla.

'That's a pity,' you say. 'Interest from someone famous could make all the difference. The Facebook page has had 1,300 likes, so we're getting somewhere, at least.'

'Jack says he can organise a flashmob,' says Sylvia. Then she adds quietly, 'but he might need some money.'

'Money? What for?' you ask. 'This project has already cost Clifton a lot of money. We have a very limited budget for promotion.'

Chapter 14

'Jack has to do some work experience as part of his final year at high school. He says that organising a flashmob is work. He says it's the job of a media co-ordinator. He wants $400.'

'What? Your son wants $400 for doing a three-minute dance with a bunch* of school friends?'

'He says they need the money for costumes.'

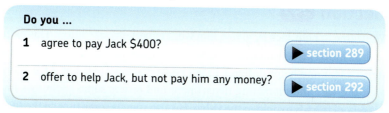

Section 291

291

⭐ You win 1 bonus point. Mark the scorecard on page 186.

You walk over to Hans and say, 'Hi, Hans! How are you?'

'Hi!' he says. 'Great, great. How are you? Did you see the dance?'

'I did!' you say. 'Where did you find that?'

'On your website,' he says. 'I was looking at the Avoca ads and then I clicked on "Other clients". It's a great idea – that dancing koala is so cute*. Dagmar loves him! But nobody knows about it.'

'I know,' you say. 'We need publicity.'

'Why don't you pay for the ad to go on TV, like with the Arrow?'

'Well, this a music video. It's three and a half minutes long. It's too long for a TV ad. We wanted it to go viral.'

'I see.'

'I'm going to ask all my contacts to promote the ad, using social media.'

'Maybe my little brother Wilhelm can help. He's well-known in Germany. DJ Willy is his name. Do you know him?'

'No, I don't Hans, sorry.'

'Oh. I guess Germany is a long way from here. Anyway, he has a show on Saturday evenings, with an audience of about three million. Maybe he could play the video?'

'Really? Could he do that?' you ask.

'Yes, why not?'

'Hans, that would be amazing.'

173

Chapter 14

'It's nothing. You did a great job with the Avoca Arrow ad. I owe you a favour[*].'

You have a very good feeling about the day as you drive down to the Clifton offices.

▶ section 287

292 Section 292

You agree to help Jack by giving him work experience at Clifton. This help will be much more valuable than $400. Jack spends two days with Eva's department and helps design a Krazy Koala costume[*]. He has a few days working with the marketing department and orders some koala toys for his school friends to hold in the video. He also spends some time in the PR[*] department and helps prepare replies to media organisations.

One morning, you get a call from Sydney TV News1. 'It's about the teenager and the dance.'

'Teenager?' you ask.

'Jack Watson is his name,' says the reporter. 'He created a Facebook event around this, er, Koala dance? His page says it's going to be the biggest flashmob in Australian history.'

'Oh, of course, Jack,' you say smiling. 'Carry on[*]!'

'This is big news for Sydney. This Facebook event has over 12,000 people listed as "attending". It says the flashmob is going to meet on the steps of the Opera House in two days' time and they are going to perform this new dance. The Gondwana Style.'

'Wow!'

'Am I speaking to the right person? Jack Watson gave me your number. He said you're his PR manager.'

'Er, that's me!' you say. You are starting to see why Jack is such hard work for his mother, Sylvia.

The reporter asks for information about Jack and the Gondwana Style dance. You can't believe your luck! The mood[*] at Clifton Creative Agency is very exciting all of a sudden. Sylvia is helping Jack to organise the event. She has hired a huge[*] music system to play the Gondwana Style song. Jack arrives at your office to collect the Krazy Koala costume to wear at the flashmob and, on the morning of the event, 15,300 people have clicked 'attending'.

▶ section 293

Chapter 14

Section 293

You catch the ferry to Sydney Opera House with Karen and John. It is three hours before the event starts, and there are already lots of people here, many of them are holding toy koalas. You find Jack near a TV truck where a reporter is interviewing people about the flashmob.

'What's going on?' you ask.

'There are a lot of people here from the TV and radio. Can you talk to them? I don't like it. I'm just here to help my mum out with her work.'

'Sure. Good luck! This is going to be fantastic.'

Twenty minutes before the event, Layla is on the stage saying, 'One, two … One, two!' into the microphone. She has agreed to start the flashmob. The area is almost full now, and you are very excited. You and Sylvia are behind the stage chatting to Jack when you hear Layla announce, 'Good afternoon, Sydney!'

There is a huge roar* from the crowd. You look out from the stage and all you can see is a sea of thousands and thousands of faces. Jack closes his eyes and takes a deep breath. His mother pats him on the back and says, 'Do it for your father. He'd be proud of you. You'll be fine, son. I love you!' Jack turns around and says to you, 'Will you dance next to me? I can't do this on my own.'

What do you say?

| 1 | 'No, you'll be fine Jack. You do it!' | ▶ section 297 |
| 2 | 'Sure.' | ▶ section 295 |

Chapter 14

294   Section 294

You, Jaspal and the team meet to talk about how to generate international interest in Gondwanaland. 'We may need to hire an external marketing agency,' says Jaspal. 'We don't have the expertise and the local market knowledge here in Sydney.'

'I could fly to London,' suggests Layla.

'I could work from home for a month and spend all day online, trying to get foreign bloggers interested in the video,' suggests John.

'I was thinking of learning Chinese,' says Eva.

Nobody, including you and Jaspal, has any good ideas. You go back to your office and look at your contacts. Maybe someone new can help you.

295   Section 295

Jack waves at the crowd and thousands of people cheer. You walk onto the stage and there is some laughter at the front.

'Are you ready Sydney?' shouts Layla. 'This is going to be Australia's biggest flashmob ever. And you, ladies and gentlemen, are a part of it. Congratulations and thank you!' The crowd roars and everybody starts to jump up and down. Suddenly, a dark cloud passes over the crowd and a strong cold wind blows your hair. Moments later, huge hailstones start falling out of the sky. The hail* gets heavier very quickly and soon lumps of ice as big as grapes are falling all around you. One hits your ear and it really hurts. You pull Jack to the side of the stage. You hear a loud bang. At first you think it is thunder, but then you realise it is the speaker system exploding. There are screams from the crowd and the helicopter flies away.

The storm lasts for five minutes, then the hail turns into cold, heavy rain. You look down the steps and see some rubbish, broken umbrellas and empty coffee cups, but the crowd has disappeared as quickly as it arrived. Jack is crying onto his mother's shoulder. 'Never mind son, you can't change the weather,' she says. You all go to a cafe in the Opera House to dry your hair and get some hot drinks.

'You mustn't think that this was a failure,' you tell Jack and the Clifton team. 'The rain ruined* the fun, but the event has been a success for Clifton. The news channels will probably report the story anyway – they love disasters. Everyone loves a disaster! You did a great job, Jack.'

Chapter 14

Jack smiles. 'Thank you, too!' he says. 'I'm going to get a great mark for my work experience project. It's going to save my schoolwork for the year. My marks haven't been great in other subjects,' he adds quietly.

▶ section 296

Section 296

296

Two weeks later, the mood* is still great at Clifton. The flashmob event got national news coverage on all the channels across the country. The 'blogosphere' is alive with talk about koalas and Gondwanaland and there is no mention of jellyfish! National radio plays the Gondwana Style song all the time and the Facebook page has had 5.4 million 'likes'. It is a marketing sensation and you know the Gondwanaland Tourism Board must be very happy.

One day you get a voicemail from Nikos.

'Hi, it's me, Nikos. Anastasia asked me to congratulate you on the Gondwana Style video. It's a big success here in Australia and it seems to be having an impact on tourism. Domestic reservations are up 25%. However, internationally, the picture isn't so good. As I'm sure you know, most of our customers come from overseas*. Apart from an unusually high level of visitors from Germany, the rest of Europe, the US and Asia are flat. We need you to generate more international interest. Remember, we paid a lot of money for an international campaign and we expect international results.'

'That will be hard,' you think.

Do you ...

| 1 | call another meeting with the team? | ▶ section 294 |
| 2 | look at your contacts and find someone new to help? | ▶ section 298 |

Section 297

297

⭐ You win 1 bonus point. Mark the scorecard on page 186.
You understand that Jack is nervous, but it will look better if he is on the stage on his own. Sometimes people need to be encouraged to believe in themselves. Jack waves at the crowd and thousands of people cheer.

177

Chapter 14

'Are you ready Sydney?' shouts Layla. 'This is going to be Australia's biggest flashmob ever. And you, ladies and gentlemen, are a part of it. Congratulations and thank you!' The crowd roars and everybody starts to jump up and down. Jack puts on the koala head. 'OK, Sydney, this is it. Three! ... two! ... one!' The music starts and 15,000 people copy the Krazy Koala on the stage. The dance moves take them from the surfboard to the bike to the jungle, the same as in the film. The event lasts three and a half minutes.

Afterwards, Layla says thank you to the crowd. Fifteen minutes later, almost all the people have gone. 'The day has been an incredible success,' you tell Jack and the Clifton team. 'It was so much better than I ever expected. I'm very impressed* with you, Jack. You've done a great job.'

Jack smiles. 'Thank you, too!' he says. 'I'm going to get a great mark for my work experience project. It's going to save my schoolwork for the year.'

Karen and Sylvia join you. 'You won't believe what Karen just told me,' says Sylvia.

'No, what?' asks Jack.

'The Gondwanaland Tourism Board has just called me,' says Karen. 'They're so pleased with the flashmob event that they want to offer you and your mum a two-week luxury holiday in Gondwanaland – all expenses paid!'

'Really? Wow!' says Jack.

'Thank you, Jack,' says Karen. 'You've earned it.'

'Oh, I'm so proud of you!' says Sylvia. She kisses Jack and hugs him.

'Aw, Mum!' he says. 'Not in front of my friends!'

 section 296

298 Section 298

Look at the Contacts section on page 186

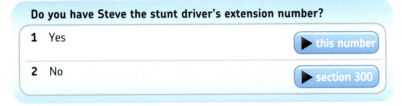

Chapter 14

Section 299

299

You stop the car and buy a coffee at the beachside cafe. You walk over to watch the old man. A little dog comes running through the crowd towards you. You can't believe it. It is Dagmar! She seems very pleased to see you. 'Dagmar!' you say. 'What are you doing here?'

The people have formed a circle and they are clapping*. You walk over to join them. You realise that it is not an old man dancing. It is Hans! And he is dancing the Gondwana Style with a couple of young surfers. You can't believe your eyes!

A few minutes later, the dance ends, people laugh and clap, and the crowd quickly disappears.

Section 300

300

You look at your contacts and phone a few people, but no one can help you. Bad luck!

You need to have Steve Freeman's extension number to get the Gondwanaland campaign international attention.

Go back to the start of the chapter 9 and speak to Steve Freeman.

Section 301

301

A week later, your phone rings. 'What have you done? We've had 50 million views of the video!'

You don't recognise* the voice at first. Then you realise it is Nikos. You have never heard him sound happy. You look at Twitter and see Livia Luz's message. You click on the link and it goes through to her blog where you see that the video of her dancing with Steve Freeman has had 17 million views and 25 million retweets* and shares.

179

Chapter 14

At last! You have done it! The Gondwana Style dance has become an international hit and it is all thanks to Steve Freeman. Within a month, Gondwanaland is one of the most popular tourist destinations on the planet. The whole world is dancing the Gondwana Style.

Ending

Section 302

The Gondwanaland Tourism Board asks Karen to organise a thank you party for everyone who helped in the campaign*. Karen books an evening at the Art Gallery of New South Wales, Sydney's most prestigious* art gallery and also a fantastic party venue*. There are lovely views over Woolloomooloo Bay as well as an impressive art collection.

The day of the party arrives. Everyone from Clifton is going, including Jack Watson. Anastasia and Nikos are going, Livia Luz and Steve Freeman are going, even Hans Fischer is going and he wants to bring Dagmar – as usual. There are about 175 people on the guest list.

Limousines* drop the guests on Art Gallery Road and they walk up the stone steps into the gallery. There are drinks and canapés, and after about an hour Karen makes an announcement. 'We are very honoured to be hosting this party on behalf of our oldest and most important client*, Gondwanaland Tourism.' Hans Fischer, who was sharing* a joke with Nikos, suddenly looks up at Karen. 'Anastasia Dimitris of the Gondwanaland Tourism Board has asked me to thank in particular the Clifton team who saved Gondwanaland.' Karen says all of your names and raises her glass to propose a toast. 'But of course, none of this could have happened without the help of some very special friends: Hans Fischer, whose brother managed to make Gondwanaland a popular destination with German holidaymakers; Jack Watson, whose fantastic flashmob event restored

Ending

Australians' confidence in the region; and last but not least Steve Freeman and Livia Luz, who danced the Gondwana Style. To all of you – a massive[*] thanks!

'We want this to be a party to remember, so to get you all in the mood Livia and Steve have agreed to dance the Gondwana Style for us this evening.'

Everybody looks up at the stage, but suddenly there is a loud bark[*] and a scream. Steve walks onto the stage, but he is limping[*]. At the side, you can see Hans point[*] a finger in Dagmar's face.

'Oh, no! Steve won't be able to dance the Gondwana Style with me tonight,' says Livia, looking at you. 'I can't do it alone. Where's that kid?' She sees Jack and he blushes. 'You're the koala, right?' she says.

'Y ... yeah,' he says.

'OK, you're going to be one of my dancers ... and you,' she says pointing to Nikos.

'No, no, I don't ...' he says, but Jack is already pulling Nikos up onto the stage. 'And you ...' she says, pointing to Layla Blackman and Pete Deng.

'Great!' says Layla.

'I'm up for it,' says Pete.

'And finally ... you,' says Livia and looks you in the eye.

With butterflies[*] in your stomach, you get up on stage next to Pete. 'Well, everyone is famous for fifteen minutes,' he says.

'Three ... two...'

'And our fifteen minutes is starting now,' you reply.

'... one! Come on everybody! Let's go!' shouts Livia.

The music booms out. Suddenly, everyone in the room starts dancing the Gondwana Style.

Your video has gone viral and your ad has not only saved Gondwanaland, it has got people dancing all over the world! Congratulations!

Look at page 186. How many bonus points did you win?

1	You have 0–6 bonus points.	▶ section 303
2	You have 7–12 bonus points.	▶ section 304
3	You have 13–16 bonus points.	▶ section 305

Ending

Section 303

Well done! You have developed two successful advertising campaigns for Clifton Creative Agency. Through your hard work and good decision-making, you have saved a company that was about to go out of business.

Over the next year, you work hard but things are not so successful. First Layla leaves the company to work as an editor on a fashion magazine. John accepts early retirement*. Finally, there is the biggest shock of all. Eva leaves to join the Young, McQuarrie and Street Agency. She becomes a partner and the company will be known as Young, McQuarrie, Street and Campano.

Without these key figures, Clifton's success comes to an end. Eventually, the Clifton directors decide to sell the company. They make a big profit*, but you don't have a job any more.

You feel sad. You did a good job but the company changed quickly and you didn't change with it. You could apply for another job in the auto industry*, but you want to find another job in advertising.

Try the maze again and see if you can win more bonus points.

Section 304

Well done! You have developed two successful advertising campaigns for Clifton Creative Agency. Through your hard work and good decision-making, you have saved a company that was about to go out of business.

Over the next year, you work hard to develop new projects. You work on a new motorbike campaign for Avoca and you spend a lot of time thinking of a new campaign for the Gondwanaland Tourism Board.

You are happy, but slightly disappointed. There are not so many good ideas coming out of team meetings. There isn't the same energy in the company as before. People don't talk as much in the corridors and staff stop wanting to share their ideas with other people.

Clifton is still in business, but the team is not as strong as in the past. You wish you had done things differently during the Avoca and Gondwanaland campaigns.

Try the maze again and see if you can win more bonus points.

Ending

305 Section 305

Well done! You have developed two successful advertising campaigns for Clifton Creative Agency. Through your hard work and good decision-making, you have saved a company that was about to go out of business.

Over the next year, you work hard to develop new projects. Everyone wants to work with you and every meeting ends with great ideas. You work on another ad that wins an ANZA Award and everyone is delighted*. The new press interest wins your company a major contract* with an airline. Suddenly, Clifton needs to recruit* new employees and the company needs to move into bigger offices.

As the year ends, Karen invites you to dinner with the other directors of the company. She announces that you have become one of the most important members of the company and you will take her old job as head of account services. She has also won a promotion and she will be the new director of the Clifton Group. Congratulations!

Your career move into advertising has been a complete success. You have become one of the biggest names in the Australian advertising industry. What next? There is a whole world of advertising waiting for you.

The end

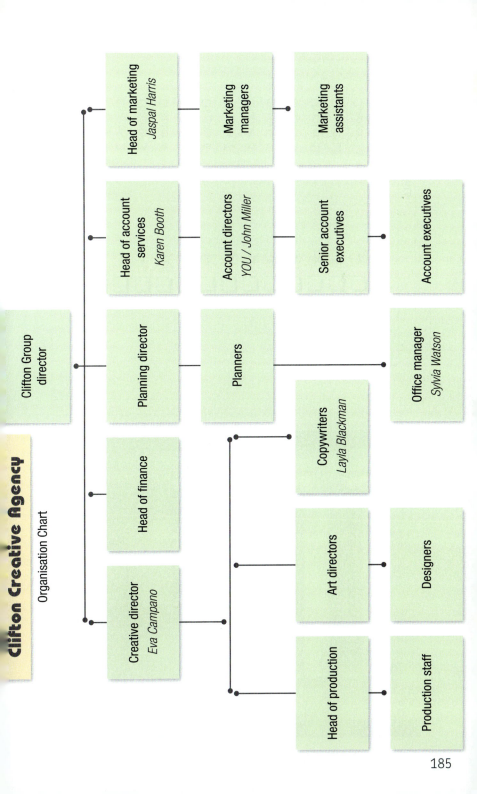

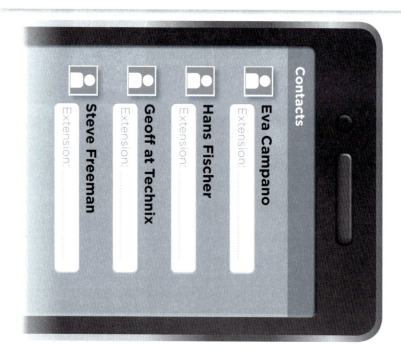

Glossary

Word	Definition
absurd	very silly, illogical, or senseless
accelerate	to go faster
accidentally	to do something without intention, or by chance
achievement	something you have done using effort or skill
acronym	the initial letters from the words in a phrase
agenda	a written plan for a meeting
aim	to direct something
air time	time on the TV or radio for programmes or advertising
allergic	having a negative reaction to particular substance
annoyed	irritated or a little angry
annoying	something that makes you irritated or a little angry
apologise	to say sorry
applicant	someone who applies for a job or place on a course
appointment	a plan to do something or meet someone at a particular time
appreciate	to see the value of something
approve	to agree that someone can do something
argue	to disagree, often in an angry way
argument	a conversation where people disagree in an angry way
assistant	someone who helps a more senior person
auto industry	all the companies that make cars and other vehicles
avoid	to keep away from someone or something

awful	very bad
awkward	difficult or uncomfortable
background	the parts of a scene which are less important
backpacker	a tourist who travels with a large bag on their back
badge	a symbol
ban	to forbid or prohibit something
bark	to make a loud noise like a dog
basement	the part of a building below ground level
benefit	an advantage or positive point
bill	a ticket showing how much you have to pay for a product or service
blush	to go red in the face when you are embarrassed
boardroom	a large meeting room
book	to reserve
brainstorming	a process where lots of people contribute their ideas
brake	to slow down or stop
brand	the image a company creates for itself and its products
bribe	to give someone money in return for a favour
brief	a summary of a situation
budget	the amount of money you have to spend
bump into	to meet someone by chance
bunch	group (informal)
butterflies	a nervous feeling
campaign	a series of actions with a specific purpose
career	a series of jobs that someone has in their life
carry on	to continue

Glossary

car-sick	to feel ill when travelling by car
cash	money in the form of notes and coins
celebrity	a famous person
chair	to lead a meeting
change your mind	to change your opinion
chase	to follow someone or something quickly
cheerful	happy or content
chew	to crush something with your teeth
claim	to say something is yours
clap	to make a noise with your hands to show your appreciation
client	a customer, usually a company
colleague	someone you work with
commission	to request and approve something
commit	to formally agree to do something
competitor	another company in the same sector
complain	say that something is wrong or you are not satisfied
concern	a worry
concerned	worried
confident	having a strong belief in yourself and your abilities
confused	unclear, unsure or mistaken
contract	an official agreement between two companies
cool	good, or fashionable, attractive and popular
cooperate	to work together
copywriter	someone who writes things for adverts and publicity
costume	clothes for a special occasion

Glossary

crew	a group of people who work together
crisis	a very serious problem
current	related to now
cute	sweet or attractive
damage	to break something
degree	the award a university gives you when you complete a course
delighted	very pleased or happy
disobedient	someone who doesn't obey the rules
doubt	a feeling of uncertainty or distrust
drop	to decrease
due	expected or planned
embarrassed	feeling shy or uncomfortable because of something you did
emphasise	to draw special attention to something
enormous	very big
envelope	a paper container, e.g. for a letter
essential	very important
eventually	in the end
examine	to look at something closely
exhausted	very tired
expect	to believe that something will happen
expire	to come to an end
fall	to decrease
fancy	to want to do something
favour	an act which helps someone
feedback	the reactions or opinions of people

Glossary

ferry	a large boat for transporting people or cars
film	to record a video
find out	to discover some information
fine	an amount of money you have to pay as a punishment
fix	to repair something that is broken, or find a solution
flood	an excess of water covering the land
forecast	a summary of the weather in the immediate future
freelancer	someone who works independently
fuel	a source of energy for a machine
furious	very angry
gesture	to make a sign with your hands
gift	a present
glad	happy or content
glare	to look at someone angrily
grab	to take something with your hands quickly
growl	to make a low angry noise
guess	to have an opinion about something without having all the evidence
gum	a sweet that you chew
hail	small balls of ice that fall like rain
hammer	a tool made of a heavy metal head and a wooden handle
handshake	a greeting when you hold and shake another person's hand
hang on	to wait for a short time
hang up	to finish a telephone conversation by putting the phone down

Glossary

harbour	a safe place where boats can stop and people can get on and off
highway	a large road
hill	a small mountain
hire	to give someone a job
hit	a success
horrified	to feel surprised in a very negative way
HR (human resources)	the department of a company which deals with the employees
huge	very big
hum	a low constant noise
ignore	to notice something is happening, but not give attention to it
immediately	in this moment, at once
impressed	having a good impression
initial	first, or early
insurance	an agreement with a company to protect a car against loss or harm
insured	having an agreement with a company to protect a car against loss or harm
jewellery	objects worn to look nice, e.g. necklaces, rings etc.
jingle	a short piece of music for an advert, usually very memorable
jogging	running to keep fit
journey	travelling between one place and another
keen	liking or wanting something
kneel	to go down and rest on your knees
lack	not having something, an absence

Glossary

landscape	an area of land with all its features
lane	a section of a road where one vehicle can travel in one direction
laptop	a computer which you can transport easily
launch	to start an activity officially
lend	to give something to someone for a period of time
liar	someone who doesn't tell the truth
licence	a document giving permission to do something
lift	to move something up using your hands or arms
limousine	a long luxurious car used for important occasions
limp	to walk with an injury in your leg
line manager	your direct boss
loan	to give something to someone for a period of time
location	a place
manners	behaviour that is considered polite
massive	very big
mate	friend (informal)
memorable	something that is easy to remember
minutes	the written summary of a meeting
misspell	to use the incorrect letters to spell a word
mistake	something you did wrong, an error
model	a type of something
mood	how you feel
mug	a large cup
mutter	to say something in a low voice so it is difficult to hear
naughty	a person or animal that behaves badly

Glossary

necklace	a type of jewellery worn around the neck
networking	meeting people to improve your professional opportunities in the future
nightmare	a terrible situation, or a bad dream
nod	to move your head up and down
nonsense	something which has no sense or meaning
nowadays	in the present, in these times
nut	a dry fruit which has a hard shell around it
off the record	unofficially
on location	doing something in a special place
open-plan	without dividing walls
optimistic	having a positive view of a situation
outsider	someone from a different industry or company
overseas	any foreign country
owner	the person who has possession of an object
PA (personal assistant)	someone who organises and helps a more senior person
pedal	something which you control with your feet
pier	a structure which extends into the sea to get on and off a boat
pitch	to present an idea to a customer
point	to signal something with your finger
PR (public relations)	how a company manages its relationship with the public
prestigious	something with a very good reputation
pretend	to give the appearance of doing something
probationary	a trial period

Glossary

profit	the money a company makes after it pays costs and taxes
properly	in the correct way
puzzled	unsure or worried about something
raise	to make something higher
receipt	a piece of paper showing how much you paid for a product or service
recognise	to identify someone or something that you have seen before
recruit	to give someone a job in a company
reference	a written report of someone's character, skills and achievements
reject	to say 'no', to not include
relieved	not feeling stressed, worried or afraid any more
reluctantly	doing something when you don't want to do it
renew	to make something effective for another period of time
repair	to make something work after it has been broken
replace	to substitute, to take the role of another person or thing
research	investigate a certain subject
resign	to tell your company that you will leave them
retirement	the period of time when you stop working because you are old
retweet	a message on Twitter which has been forwarded
reverse	to go backwards
ridiculous	very silly, illogical, or senseless
risk	a possible danger
roar	to make a very loud sound

Glossary

ruined — broken or destroyed

run — to manage or lead

rush — to go quickly

sack — to tell someone to leave a company

scary — something which produces fear

schedule — a plan of when to do a series of actions

scout — someone who observes and reports things

scratch — to move your fingers or nails on a surface

script — the words for a TV or radio programme

seagull — a type of seabird

seek — to look for

shade — an area which is not in direct sunlight

shake — to move from one side to another

share — to divide something equally, or to pass information to other people

shocked — surprised in a negative way

slang — informal or colloquial language

slogan — a phrase associated with a product

small talk — making polite conversation

smoothly — without any problems

snack — a small piece of food eaten between meals

snorkel — a tube used to breath when your head is under water

soap opera — a TV or radio programme about the lives of many characters

spectacular — incredible, amazing, very good

speech — a formal talk

speeding — illegally driving too fast

spell — to say the letters which form a word

Glossary

sponsor	a company that pays to broadcast a TV programme to advertise a product
staff	a group of employees that work at an organisation
stare	to look at something or someone in an intense way
stationery	items used in an office, e.g. pens, papers, envelopes etc.
steam	water in the form of gas or vapour
stereotype	a simplified and often false concept which is widely believed
stick	to put something somewhere (informal)
sting	the form of defence used by animals such as bees, wasps, jellyfish etc.
stressed	to feel tense or psychologically pressured
stressful	causing tension or pressure
stunt	a dangerous act which attracts attention
suburb	a residential area of a city
suburban	someone living in a residential area of a city
sunbathe	to lie in the sun
sunstroke	illness caused by exposure to too much sunlight
suntan	a darker skin colour caused by exposure to sunlight
support	help or encouragement
survey	the impression or opinion of a group of people
swap	to exchange one thing for another
sweat	to release a liquid when you are hot, to perspire
swipe	to move something quickly through a machine
tap	to hit a surface with your fingertips
target	a desired group
terrible	very bad

197

Glossary

torch	a light which can be carried in the hand
track	a road without a hard surface
trendy	fashionable, attractive and popular
tuxedo	a suit for special occasions worn with a bowtie
tweet	to send a message on Twitter
update	to add new information to reflect the current situation
upset	sad and a little angry
venomous	a poisonous animal
venue	a place for an event
vet's	a place where animals are looked after medically
voice-over	the voice of an off-screen narrator, especially in an advert
warn	to say the bad consequences of an action
waste	to use something unproductively
wave	to move your arms or hands to greet someone or attract attention
weak	not powerful, or not good
wetsuit	a special suit which keeps you warm when you are under water
wildlife	undomesticated animals
wrap	to completely cover something
youth hostel	a cheap and basic place to stay when travelling

58 St Aldates
Oxford
OX1 1ST
United Kingdom

© 2014, Santillana Educación, S.L. / Richmond

Publisher: Ruth Goodman
Editor(s): David Cole-Powney, Carole Hughes, Zanna Taylor
Digital Publisher: Luke Baxter
Senior Digital Editor: Belen Fernandez
Software Developers: Avallain
Digital Management: Haremi
Design Manager: Lorna Heaslip
Logo Design: Russell Hrachovec at compoundEye
Design & Layout: Lorna Heaslip, Dave Kuzmicki
Picture Editor: Magdalena Mayo

ISBN: 978-84-668-1851-3

First edition: 2014

Printed in Spain
DL: M-8865-2014

No unauthorised copying
All rights reserved. No part of this book may be reproduced, stored in a retrieval system or transmitted in any form by any means, electronic, mechanical, photocopying, recording or otherwise, without the prior permission in writing of the Publisher.

Photographs:
iStockphoto; ARCHIVO SANTILLANA

Illustrations:
Aleix Pons Oliver, Chee Yong c/o Lemonade Illustration Agency

Audio:
Motivation Sound Studios, www.motivationsound.co.uk; Sound Jay, www.soundjay.com

Every effort has been made to trace the holders of copyright before publication. The Publisher will be pleased to rectify any errors or omissions at the earliest opportunity.